THE (SLIGHTLY DISTRACTED)
WOMAN'S GUIDE TO LIVING WITH
AN ADULT ADHD DIAGNOSIS

by the same author

The Educator's Experience of Pathological Demand Avoidance
An Illustrated Guide to Pathological Demand Avoidance and Learning
Laura Kerbey
Illustrated by Eliza Fricker
ISBN 978 1 83997 696 4
eISBN 978 1 83997 698 8

The Teen's Guide to Pathological Demand Avoidance
Laura Kerbey
Foreword by Dr Julia Woollatt
Illustrated by Eliza Fricker
ISBN 978 1 80501 183 5
eISBN 978 1 80501 184 2

of related interest

ADHD Girls to Women
Getting on the Radar
Lotta Borg Skoglund
ISBN 978 1 80501 054 8
eISBN 978 1 80501 055 5

ADHD an A-Z
Figuring it Out Step by Step
Leanne Maskell
ISBN 978 1 83997 385 7
eISBN 978 1 83997 386 4

The (Slightly Distracted) Woman's Guide to Living with an Adult ADHD Diagnosis

Laura Kerbey
ILLUSTRATED BY ELIZA FRICKER

Jessica Kingsley Publishers
London and Philadelphia

First published in Great Britain in 2025 by Jessica Kingsley Publishers
An imprint of John Murray Press

1

Copyright © Laura Kerbey 2025
Illustrations Copyright © Eliza Fricker 2025

The right of Laura Kerbey to be identified as the Author of the Work has been asserted by her in accordance with the Copyright, Designs and Patents Act 1988.

All rights reserved. No part of this publication may be reproduced, stored in a retrieval system, or transmitted, in any form or by any means without the prior written permission of the publisher, nor be otherwise circulated in any form of binding or cover other than that in which it is published and without a similar condition being imposed on the subsequent purchaser.

A CIP catalogue record for this title is available from the British Library and the Library of Congress

ISBN 978 1 80501 208 5
eISBN 978 1 80501 209 2

Printed and bound in Great Britain by Clays Ltd

Jessica Kingsley Publishers' policy is to use papers that are natural, renewable and recyclable products and made from wood grown in sustainable forests. The logging and manufacturing processes are expected to conform to the environmental regulations of the country of origin.

Jessica Kingsley Publishers
Carmelite House
50 Victoria Embankment
London EC4Y 0DZ

www.jkp.com

John Murray Press
Part of Hodder & Stoughton Ltd
An Hachette Company

The authorised representative in the EEA is Hachette Ireland,
8 Castlecourt Centre, Dublin 15, D15 XTP3, Ireland (email: info@hbgi.ie)

This book is dedicated to Luna, the best impulse purchase I ever made, and the one I will always miss the most.

Acknowledgements

I cannot express my gratitude enough to you, the incredible women who contributed to this book, which would not have been possible without you. It has been such a privilege to read your words and share your experiences. You made me feel less weird, and I know that so many other women will benefit from reading about your experiences, and be validated by them.

To my ADHD girl gang: Amy, Andrea L, Heather, Karen and Lisa. I am very grateful to have you all in my life. Also, to Andrea H, Chloe, Lucy and Sarah for always being there for me when I have needed you.

As always, thank you to Eliza for your brilliant illustrations, friendship, laughs, support and most excellent time spent together.

Thank you to Siân for all your help with the referencing and quotes in the book. I literally could not have done this without you!

Finally, thank you to Sean and Abbie at JKP for your support and patience with this book.

Contents

Acknowledgements 7

Introduction 11

Ch 1: **Childhood and Education** 29

Ch 2: **Parenting** 49

Ch 3: **ADHD, Hormones and Menopause** 74

Ch 4: **Rejection Sensitive Dysphoria and Imposter Syndrome** 90

Ch 5: **Work and Career** 114

Ch 6: **How to Manage the Ups and Downs of ADHD and Mental Health** 141

Ch 7: **Friendships and Relationships** 168

Ch 8: **Impulsivity and Impatience** 184

Ch 9: **Special Interests, Obsessions and Random Collections** 199

Ch 10: **Shopping (and Other Addictions)** 212

Ch 11: **Dropping the Disorder and Reframing My ADHD** 235

References 248

Introduction

LAZY

CLUMSY

STUPID

FORGETFUL

ANNOYING

WEIRD

a bit much

Disorganized

OVERSENSITIVE

WALKING DISASTER

I received my ADHD diagnosis at the grand age of 46. My diagnosis was thorough, lengthy (therefore not always ADHD-friendly) and private (therefore not cheap, but still significantly less than a French Bulldog, and about the same price as a Ragdoll cat, which have been some of my better ADHD impulse buys).

My diagnosis is, without doubt, one of the most important and defining moments of my life. I have started to think of my life in two parts, BD (Before Diagnosis) and AD (After Diagnosis). In my "BD life", I regularly thought of myself as:

- Clumsy
- Stupid
- Forgetful
- Annoying
- Disorganized
- Oversensitive
- Lazy
- And generally, a bit of a walking disaster.

I am not alone in feeling like this, as the quotes from the other women who contributed to this book will testify.

WALKING DISASTER

"Pre-diagnosis, I thought I was broken, scatty, 'too much', unreliable, a walking disaster, chaos on two feet."

KYRA

INTRODUCTION

STUPID

"I felt as if I was broken and in need of fixing.
I remember asking for a new brain for Christmas
year after year as mine just didn't work the way I felt
it should."

JO

FORGETFUL

"I always felt a sense of urgency/impending doom – a
feeling of needing to 'get everything done' (but still not
managing it) – for no actual discernible reason."

KATIE

Disorganized

"I thought I was unreliable, believing that I just let
people down all of the time and couldn't be trusted.
As an intelligent and competent adult, it is truly
devastating to know that people often just see you as a
series of character flaws."

IRIS

I don't think I ever really felt good enough in many aspects
of my life, which led to masking, imposter syndrome

and, at times, crippling anxiety. I was racing through life, anticipating the next f*ck up, the next thing I would damage or destroy through my inability to focus and just generally get my shit together. Again, it is clear that I am not alone in thinking this way.

CLUMSY

"I used to think of myself as 'The Goddess of the Faux Pas'. I felt like I was always impulsively doing or saying the wrong things, and I always felt like I was somehow missing details others were picking up on, like, I didn't know the 'secret handshake'."

STEPHANIE

Disorganized

"I was intelligent, but I would always miss, forget or mess up simple tasks. I was great at taking on big projects, and paralysed by the inability to take one item back to the shop. Other girls and women always seemed so well groomed and put together, but I just couldn't match it. Mainly because I couldn't give sufficient time and attention to it."

DEBORAH

INTRODUCTION

I decided to seek a diagnosis during the Covid-19 pandemic. As a positive, this was a time when I really started to form more friendships and connections with other neurodivergent women through my work, and realized that I had much in common with them.

But as a negative, this was also a time when our lives were turned upside down, and many of us who were already struggling with our executive functioning and the day-to-day management of life had even more challenges to face, such as home-schooling our children (I gave up, and I am a teacher!), working from home, trying to get an online shopping delivery slot and planning food shops for three weeks ahead, as well as finding elusive goods such as toilet rolls!

(How so many people found the time to bake banana bread and sourdough loaves during lockdown will always remain a mystery to me, although I did bake a very interesting baked bean cake after impulsively buying the biggest can of baked beans you have ever seen. It was actually very nice, as agreed by the people I managed to persuade to try it!)

This unprecedented time of life seemed to create a tsunami of diagnoses of autism and ADHD in many women. Women who, like me, at best were seen by themselves or by others as those previously mentioned negatives.

STUPID

"I wish my neurodiversity had been picked up on at university, or during all the counselling I underwent in my twenties and thirties (and forties!)."

KATIE

LAZY

"Before I realized I was ADHD, I always just assumed I was lazy. Why was it that I could get loads done and work solidly for five hours on a task one day, but then not be able to move from the sofa to do so much as take my plates out to the sink the next? I just always thought of myself as chronically lazy, like, why can't I motivate myself to have a clean and tidy house like everyone else?"

AMY

Disorganized

"I think that neurodivergent thing of not really knowing how things are done and feeling like there's a 'secret club', that unless you're a member of it, you won't get to know all the important life information."

KATIE

INTRODUCTION

OVERSENSITIVE

"I thought I was incapable. A frequent intrusive thought was 'Why can't I do this when everyone else can?' I thought I was irrationally anxious and I felt locked into one level; although I knew that wasn't my place in life, I knew I could attain better, but didn't have a 'key' to the next level up."

MICHELLE

STUPID

"Firstly, I feel it is so important to have an understanding of your own ADHD brain and how it works. For women in particular, the ways our ADHD manifests are only recently being talked about. The executive functioning difficulties, RSD [rejection sensitive dysphoria] and fatigue can be so debilitating and the masking we tend to do means it goes unrecognized."

AMY

In 2024, the charity ADHD UK estimated that there were 1.9 million adults in the UK who had ADHD but did not currently have a diagnosis. That is absolutely **huge**!!!

I believe that a lot of medical professionals do not understand the way that ADHD presents in women.

If a parent took their child to a GP and told them that the child was struggling to focus, concentrate, regulate their mood, organize themselves, etc., I would hope most GPs would think about ADHD. Unfortunately, I don't believe that many GPs, even today, would automatically consider ADHD if an adult woman presented with these symptoms.

When I went to the GP in my late twenties, as I was struggling with all the above, I was diagnosed with "domestic stress". Yes, you did read that right.

> A study by Ulrika Klefsjö *et al.* in 2021 stated that "with the exception of girls with hyperactivity disorders, more boys than girls are referred for behavioral problems in school age. ADHD in girls is more often identified in adolescence or in adulthood [6]. Parents and teachers seem often to fail to identify ADHD symptoms in girls, while the girls themselves report ADHD symptoms" (p.301). The study also found that "Girls with ADHD seem more often to be referred to CAP [Child and Adolescent Psychiatry] due to emotional problems, be older than boys when they first visit the clinic and older when they receive the diagnosis. More visits to CAP were required for girls before the diagnosis was established" (p.305).

CLUMSY

"Having been diagnosed autistic and ADHD in my forties, I have spent a lot of time reflecting back on my childhood experiences and wondering what might have been different had my neurodivergence been identified when I was young. Perhaps the thing that fills me with most sadness is that the 'signs' were all there. The people and professionals around me were all noticing my difficulties and behaviours, which we now know to be due to my neurotype, but because it was the '80s and I didn't present like the text book (male) autistic ADHDer, it was totally missed."

RACHAEL

In January 2021, an article by Lilly Constance, published in *ADDitude Magazine*, stated:

> by adulthood, most women with ADHD have at least one comorbid disorder that can complicate the ADHD symptom picture, including:
>
> - anxiety (25–40% of people with ADHD have an anxiety disorder)
> - mood disorders
> - dysregulated eating (bulimia is most common)
> - externalizing disorders, like oppositional defiant disorder (ODD) or conduct disorder (mostly found in women with impulsive-type ADHD)

- personality disorders, like borderline personality disorder (BPD).

There are many myths about ADHD, but I think one of the most common and unhelpful is that it just affects "naughty boys".

> According to the ADHD UK website in 2023, "In the UK, a research survey of 10,438 children between the ages of 5 and 15 years found that 3.62% of boys and 0.85% of girls had ADHD. Global prevalence is considered to be between 2 and 7% with an average of 5%... Regarding the gender split (roughly 4:1 boys:girls) there is an active discussion about whether female ADHD is under-diagnosed and if so the reasons for that."

I strongly feel that the way we recognize and diagnose ADHD in children is heavily biased to the way that boys present, which means that there are thousands of young girls who are growing up just as I did, being and feeling misunderstood, and developing negative feelings about themselves, their ability and their worth.

Whatever the "official" statistics, I still believe they are missing a huge number of women, and sadly these women are probably still suffering as a result.

INTRODUCTION

> Of course, the presentation of ADHD changes as we get older. According to the Clinical Knowledge Summaries from NICE (National Institute for Health and Care Excellence), between 3% and 4% of adults have ADHD (NICE 2024).

> NICE's Clinical Knowledge Summaries (2024) break ADHD down into three subtypes – inattentive, hyperactive-impulsive and combined:
>
> - 20–30% of people diagnosed have inattentive subtype ADHD
> - 15% of people have hyperactive-impulsive subtype ADHD
> - 50–75% of cases have combined subtype ADHD.

I have been diagnosed with "combined subtype" ADHD, which is the same as my son.

I don't like the "deficit" or "disorder" part of "attention deficit hyperactivity disorder" because I don't feel deficient or disordered; my brain, which is sometimes amazing, just works a bit differently to others.

I also think that the term "attention deficit hyperactivity disorder" is really inaccurate. I don't have a deficit of attention. The opposite is true – I have too much attention!

My brain never stops; it's like permanently having a radio on in the background in my house. Sometimes the "tunes/thoughts" are a bit annoying, sometimes they are just background noise/thoughts, and then there will be the occasional banger/incredible brain wave!!

In the last ten years, I have set up and run two successful businesses, and this is my third published book. I couldn't do this without my amazing ADHD brain, without my ideas, creativity, passion and ability to hyperfocus. Everything I have achieved is largely because of my ADHD, not despite it. It's no wonder so many entrepreneurs have ADHD!

Without doubt, the most important part of understanding and accepting my ADHD diagnosis has been the connections I have made with other neurodivergent women – my "neurodivergent squad". I now realize that most of the people I gravitate to are also neurodivergent, because these are the people I can be truly authentic with, the people who helped me to realize that I am not:

- Clumsy
- Weird
- A bit much
- Stupid
- Forgetful
- Annoying
- Disorganized
- Oversensitive
- And generally, a bit of a walking disaster.

INTRODUCTION

So, if you are here, reading this, because you have recently been diagnosed with ADHD, or you have recently started self-identifying, then welcome to the wonderful "ADHD Club". I hope you find this book valuable and validating. I hope, like me, you will begin to realize that you are neither deficient nor disordered. You are an amazing woman, with a brain that works differently.

The most important aspect of this book is that it doesn't just feature **my** experiences of living with ADHD; this book is filled with anecdotes and experiences of other amazing women who are late-diagnosed or self-identifying ADHDers. The ages of the women who contributed to this book range from mid-thirties to late sixties, and they come from countries across the world. When they sent me their words, I sometimes laughed, I sometimes got emotional, but I always felt so validated. I felt less weird, less alone. I so hope you feel the same when you read this book.

At the end of each chapter, there is a box for you to record any "lightbulb" moments or notes that you may have when you are reading.

So, strap in and enjoy this journey. We may go off-track sometimes, but I hope that by the time you finish this book, you will have a greater understanding of yourself. I hope you will feel less weird, less broken, and that you will have a better understanding of yourself. I hope, when you have finished reading, you can be kinder to yourself, and I hope that, like me, you will feel proud to be an ADHDer.

If you are new to ADHD, there are some terms you may not have heard of that you will see reoccurring throughout this book.

Masking: Disguising or deliberately hiding or compensating your ADHD symptoms to try to fit in in, environments where you do not feel comfortable or safe being your authentic self. When masking, you may also copy others or take cues from them to try to blend in.

Imposter syndrome: A term coined by psychologists in the 1970s to describe a pattern of thinking or behaviour where an individual doubts their achievements and abilities and has a fear of being exposed as a fake or a fraud.

Rejection sensitive dysphoria (RSD): A term that describes the significant emotional impact of perceived rejection or criticism from others.

INTRODUCTION

WHAT ELSE COULD HELP?

✓ If you are reading this book because you suspect you may be ADHD, and think a diagnosis would be helpful, please don't put off seeking one.

✓ If you are in the UK, you have a legal right to choose your mental healthcare provider. You can request an assessment of ADHD by going to your GP and asking for an NHS diagnosis via Right to Choose. This means that you can get a referral to a private assessment service, but for free – although there may still be a wait.

✓ If you decide to go private, you could be seen much quicker, but make sure you do your research and that the service has a good understanding of ADHD and women.

✓ Finally, self-identification as an ADHDer **is valid**!!! You do not need to get a diagnosis to "make" you ADHD. If you self-identify as ADHD and you know that this is helpful to you, you may not need a diagnosis. As someone once said to me, "You don't need an assessment to determine your sexuality, so why should we have to have an assessment to determine our neurotype?"

✓ Try not to be surprised or upset if not everyone validates your diagnosis. When I got mine, a few people responded with "Really? Aren't we all a bit ADHD, though?" This was mainly from neurotypical people who didn't understand.

Useful links

It may be helpful to listen to some podcasts dedicated to adult ADHDing to realize you are not alone. Here are some suggestions:

- "ADHD for Smart Ass Women" with Tracy Otsuka,[1] celebrating the strengths and gifts of women with ADHD
- "The Adulting with ADHD Podcast" with Sarah Snyder,[2] offering tips and strategies for managing ADHD in everyday life
- "Women & ADHD" with Katy Weber,[3] exploring the personal stories and experiences of women with ADHD
- "ADHD Women's Wellbeing Podcast" with Kate Moryoussef,[4] focusing on the wellbeing and mental health of women with ADHD.

There are also some fantastic Instagram accounts by women with ADHD, who share relatable content:

- @authenticallyadhd[5]
- @go_adhd[6]

---

1 www.tracyotsuka.com/podcasts
2 https://adultingwithadhd.libsyn.com
3 www.womenandadhd.com
4 www.adhdwomenswellbeing.co.uk/adhd-podcast?offset=1712668320488
5 https://authenticallyadhd.com
6 www.instagram.com/go_adhd

INTRODUCTION

- @mollys_adhd_mayhem[7]
- @adhdhustlers[8]
- @adhd_love_[9]
- @adhdelite[10]

---

7 www.instagram.com/mollys_adhd_mayhem
8 www.instagram.com/Adhdhustlers
9 www.adhd-love.co.uk
10 www.instagram.com/adhdelite

Chapter One

Childhood and Education

When I look back on my childhood, it is always summer. I have lots of very happy memories of playing outside, being with my brothers and friends, and riding my horse. Yes, I know that makes me sound very privileged!

I was a very active child. The nickname my parents gave me when I was tiny was "Weeble" as I was always charging about and would "wobble but never fall down".[1] I used to watch TV upside down with my legs over the back of the sofa, and generally never stopped! I'm sure many of you will recognize similar active traits in yourselves.

"I had very little ability to assess for danger, or perhaps I did know that activities were dangerous, but I did them anyway. I constantly put my body on the line. When racing my dad and older sister, I dove into a garage full of hard objects such as bikes, mower, wood and tools, in order to try and beat them."

SARAH B

Like many neurodivergent children, I found primary school much easier than secondary school. But I remember, every time I was out with my mum, if we bumped into one of her friends and they asked if I was enjoying school, my mum would answer for me and say, "Oh she loves school, don't you?!" and I would smile and nod my head, while thinking, "No I don't!"

In school, I would regularly ask to go to the toilet as I found staying in the classroom for long periods of time very difficult, and was clearly self-regulating. (I still use the toilet as an excuse for a break in adulthood.) Many ADHD women

---

1   See https://flashbak.com/45-years-later-weebles-wobble-but-they-dont-fall-down-63318

I've spoken to have shared their negative feelings about their experiences of school.

"I remember being so painfully bored all of the time. I would spend nearly every single day deep in a funk of near-total sensory deprivation and not understanding why everyone else seemed to not feel the same way. My teachers would say things like 'Only boring people are bored!' and you start to internalize that self-hatred after a while...maybe I am just a shit human being?! So you try hard to be a better and more shiny version of yourself, but it presents to others as 'too much' and 'inauthentic'."

IRIS

"At primary school, I was known as the 'weird' kid and didn't really have any good friends until Year 6 when I connected with two other 'weird' girls. I was labelled a show-off by the kids and a chatterbox by the teachers. So much so that a teacher once told me they wanted to tape up my mouth. I said, 'No problem' and got the Sellotape® and taped my mouth shut in front of the whole class. When I ripped it off, my lips bled everywhere."

GEMMA

I would also describe myself as "cleverly naughty"! My best friend and I would regularly get up to lots of mischief, such as hoisting the school flag up the pole and "accidentally" forgetting to secure it, so the head teacher had to climb up on to the roof to retrieve it!

"Accidentally" dropping jars of paint in the classroom so that they smashed and sprayed paint everywhere! (This was on the night of parents' evening, and I had actually been tasked with tidying up the classroom while the other children did PE. My teacher went MAD when he came back in the room and saw that it was awash with blue paint!)

"Accidentally" throwing hand soap at the newly painted toilet walls so that they were stripped of their new coat. (Can you imagine what that soap was doing to our hands!?)

"Accidental" occurrences appear to be a common theme among women with ADHD.

"My funniest moment came in Sex Ed, when my brain became fixated on the word 'flaccid'. Can't think of it even now at almost 40 without descending into giggles. After a warning to stop giggling and 'grow up and stop distracting the class', I got sent out until I could compose myself – so guess who was outside most of that lesson?!"

KYRA

CHILDHOOD AND EDUCATION

Despite my mischievousness, I was rarely caught, the finger of blame often directed at others. However, I felt very conflicted during my time at school – clearly getting up to mischief as it was exciting, fun and dopamine-producing. But I was also terrified of getting into trouble!!

"I was most commonly described as a chatterbox, a big mouth, bossy and attention-seeking. I never felt any of these were fair assessments of my personality, but I had no way to challenge them internally or externally. I was popular with a lot of my peers because I was fun and had lots of ideas of things to do. Some adults liked my liveliness and spark, but many disapproved and not so subtly recoiled. I've lived all my life with a sense of being 'too much' for a lot of people."

DEBORAH

My school reports often mentioned that I was a chatterbox, and that I "could do better" if I talked less and focused more.

> Psychiatrist and author William W. Dodson wrote a paper in 2016 where he estimated that by the age of 12, children who have ADHD will have received 20,000 more negative messages from parents, teachers and other adults than their friends and siblings who do not have ADHD.

Is it any wonder that so many girls with ADHD grow up experiencing low self-esteem, rejection sensitive dysphoria (RSD) and self-doubt?!

"My school reports are full of phrases like 'Capable, but needs to learn to focus', 'Has a tendency to let herself get distracted', 'Needs to spend less time chatting and more time working'. It's such a shame (and also pretty frustrating) that no one ever thought to ask why?"

RACHAEL

"Primary school was difficult. I struggled to stay focused if the topic did not interest me. I could not wait to be called on, especially if I knew the answer, and had difficulty restraining myself from calling out. Sitting still anywhere was hard, and my mind wandered constantly. Play time was not long enough!"

SARAH B

Because I was considered "bright", I felt a huge amount of expectation on me. And I never really felt I lived up to these expectations.

I thought of myself as a "B+" grade kind of girl. I never

thought of myself as being "excellent" or "exceptional" at anything. I never thought of myself as "good enough" – my imposter syndrome had begun.

I struggled with homework, often leaving it to the last moment, and remember once being so worried about losing my reading card that I stayed up most of the night trying to forge my parents' signature on the back of an old Christmas card, as I was so scared of going back into school without "proof" that I was reading, which was ironic as I was usually awake most of the night under the covers with a torch reading. I just always forgot to ask for "proof" from my mum or dad.

Leaving things to the last minute and risking overwhelm/burnout is something that most people with ADHD are familiar with, and it doesn't necessarily end at childhood.

I would get incredibly anxious about tests. We had a spelling or maths test every Friday at my middle school, and I was so scared of doing badly that I would often feign illness on a Friday morning. No one ever seemed to notice the pattern!

When I was about seven, I went to a friend's gymnastics party and was "spotted" by one of the coaches. This resulted in me becoming a competitive gymnast. Although I think the physical aspect of gymnastics was good for me as it was so hard for me to sit still, I would also get extremely anxious about training and competitions, and was terrified of one of my coaches.

"I vividly remember not being about to concentrate at secondary school on anything that required sustained thinking. I just couldn't focus in the school environment. I always put off my GCSE coursework until the last possible moment, and usually pulled all-nighters to get the coursework finished by the deadline. I did well academically at school, but it was very stressful as I felt terrible when I had deadlines and would feel guilty that I couldn't get started. Friends and teachers thought I found the work easy as I got really good results, but in reality, I found it overwhelming and difficult."

MIRIAM

I felt a lot of pressure to do well at gymnastics and began to hate it. I never felt as good as the rest of the squad, and was actually relieved when I was diagnosed with a knee problem, which meant I had to give it up.

These traits are so clearly ADHD, but were not identified at the time. You may recognize many of those things from your own childhood. I would imagine that there are probably hundreds and thousands of women who are ADHD who were like me in school, and it probably never occurred to their teachers or their parents that they were neurodivergent.

Forty years ago, ADHD was not even properly recognized in boys, let alone girls. I am sure we were all described as shy, awkward, chatterboxes, naughty, lazy, daydreamers or similar, and these false descriptions from others led to so much confusion, low self-esteem and self-doubt in so many of us with ADHD that can only have had an impact on us as we journeyed through our childhood and beyond.

Like many neurodivergent children, the move from primary to secondary school was awful. I absolutely hated it. I know from my work that so many neurodivergent children struggle with that transition. I look back at my time in secondary school and feel nothing but negativity about this period of my life; it was a miserable time.

When I look back, I feel so sorry for my younger self and the things she had to endure. (I also still remember with horror the time when my knickers fell down, completely unintentionally – on this occasion – as the elastic had gone on them. It happened as I ran across the playground to fetch my PE kit from my locker, as my lack of organization meant I had forgotten to take it to my PE lesson. Luckily, no one saw – I don't think – but I still have nightmares about it!!)

I remember on my first day in secondary school, sitting in my new form room next to a girl called Tracey. Tracey was petite and pretty, and looked very neat and tidy in her uniform. Sitting next to her, I felt gauche and scruffy. (Having curly hair in the '80s, before the plethora of hair products that are now available, meant I always looked like I had been dragged through a hedge backwards!)

I noticed how Tracey placed her ruler, pens and pencils on her desk, and I copied her exactly. I realize now that I survived many situations by taking my cues from others, not able or confident enough to do "my own thing" or just be "me".

"Secondary school was an utterly awful time for me and has scarred me immeasurably for the rest of my life to date. It is quite painful talking and thinking about it, but I need to talk about it to help prevent others in the future going through what I went through, because of undiagnosed neurodivergence."

KATIE

I didn't realize it at the time, but I was masking, and taking my cues from those around me in a desperate attempt to be like them. As I will discuss in many chapters of this book, masking became something I would do throughout my childhood, teens and into adulthood, to hide or cover up my differences as I desperately tried to fit in.

I was separated from my best friend when I started secondary school. She seemed to slot in really well and soon found a new group of friends. I missed her dreadfully and was desperate to fit in elsewhere. I was in awe of the "Cool Girls" in my school. I was not pretty or cool enough to

CHILDHOOD AND EDUCATION

be part of their clique, but, desperate to ingratiate myself with them, I became their "gopher".

"What makes sense to me now is the constant anxiety and self-doubt that I carried with me, the pervasive rejection sensitive dysphoria, which was camouflaged by my fawning and people pleasing. I wish I could tell my younger self that it wasn't necessary to put myself in social situations with the cool crowd, with girls who clearly didn't like me that much, and tell myself I didn't have to fawn as much as I did, or just accept being the occasional butt of their teasing."

MICHELE

"I found my teen years to be the most difficult. This was due to people pleasing by giving my 'friends' my lunch money for cigarettes. They would then conveniently disappear, and I would spend the rest of lunchtime in the toilets, starving and too embarrassed to be seen wandering around the school grounds by myself."

LESLEY

The "Cool Girls" were too cool and important to line up for their own break-time snacks or lunch, so they would give me their money and I would line up in the canteen for them, and then go back to give their food to them, grateful for any acknowledgement from them, any crumb of appreciation of friendship; my need to "people please" allowed myself to be treated this way.

As girls with ADHD, it seems common that we were the victims of unkind, unwanted and bullying behaviours from our peers at school.

One of the worst things that happened to me at secondary school was when one of the "Cool Girls" told me that a much older boy "fancied me". Let's call him Kevin. Kevin, in his tight school trousers, white socks, black slip-on shoes and Simon Le Bon hairstyle, was the object of many girls' affections. I was actually mortified that Kevin "fancied me" as I was far more interested in Darren (God, these '80s names!). Darren was the naughtiest boy in my year, who didn't appear to know I existed.

Kevin would come and "chat me up" in the playground, and I would stand awkwardly trying to make conversation with him, feeling mortified, blushing furiously, and embarrassed that I didn't reciprocate his feelings for me, while the "Cool Girls" looked on, sniggering. I thought they were just jealous.

I would cycle home from school, and as I cycled past the older children walking home, they would shout at me, "Where's Kevin?" and burst out laughing.

Kevin would seek me out, paying me compliments and once telling me my hair was like Carol Decker's from T'Pau. Eventually, after weeks of being followed around by Kevin, with the "Cool Girls" looking on enviously, I decided I had to put him out of his misery. My heart was set on Darren, despite the fact he still wasn't aware of my existence.

Eager not to upset Kevin, I sought the advice of another girl in my year. She was going out with an older boy who was in Kevin's year, and I thought she would be the best person to advise me on how to let Kevin down gently. As I started to explain my predicament, she interrupted me and said, "Laura, Kevin doesn't like you. It's just a big joke."

I was absolutely mortified. Not that bloody Kevin didn't fancy me, but that I was clearly the butt of some enormous joke that it felt like the whole school was in on. I honestly don't remember how I reacted or responded, probably because it was actually really traumatic for me.

When I think back on this horrible experience and how I was treated by some of my peers at school, I feel a mixture of embarrassment and anger, and it raises many questions in my mind:

- Why did I let myself be treated so badly by others?
- Why was I singled out like this by others?
- Why was I such an easy target for this type of emotional bullying?

Let's face it, teenage girls can be pretty vile, particularly in a pack, and I think the "Cool Girls" in my school noticed I was different in some way, and they noticed my desperation to fit in and be like them. Because I would never treat others like this, it would never have occurred to me that this type of bullying would happen.

During this time, I didn't really know who I was or how to just be myself, and perhaps they knew that I would never have the guts to stand up for myself, as I would fawn so much around them. I think I was probably considered a bit "weird" at school, but I didn't realize at the time that this was how others perceived me.

> If you were bulled at school, then you are not alone. For girls with ADHD, it seems common that we were the victims of unkind, unwanted and bullying behaviours from our peers at school. Research published by *ADDitude Magazine* in 2021 stated that children with ADHD are almost four times more likely to be a victim of bullying compared to their neurotypical peers (Constance 2021).

In short, that secondary school was absolute hell for me at times. I felt like I had no friends, I found the environment overwhelming, the classes of more than 30 children meant I got lost in the mix, the homework was almost impossible to stay on top of, and I felt like there was no one to ask for help. I woke up every school day with a feeling of absolute dread.

"Very early on in Year 7, the French teacher made me her 'pet', and this started off the bullying. I ended up failing at French totally as I became a bit naughty in the French teacher's class (she had absolutely no class control), and went from being the brightest student in that class to scraping a CSE Grade 2 in French. I did this in order to be accepted, as I realized that it was not 'cool' to be clever."

KATIE

My teachers either seemed to be completely unaware of me or would tell me off for forgetting my homework, talking or not concentrating. I didn't feel that they had the time or the patience to explain things to me, and I once got into a lot of trouble when a friend did my maths homework for me. (Although really grateful for her support, I feel she could have spent a bit more effort on changing her handwriting! The fact that we both got the same questions wrong was a bit of a giveaway too!)

I left that secondary school shortly after "Kevin Gate". My parents could see how deeply unhappy I was, my grades had started to really slide, and so I was enrolled in a very small and nurturing private girls' school just down the road from my secondary school. Although a million times better than the secondary school I was at, I never really felt that I fitted in there, but I will always be eternally grateful to my parents for getting me out of what was a hellhole for me, and the considerable financial sacrifices they made to do so.

I still struggled with focus and attention, often gazing out of the window and daydreaming, but with much smaller classes and much kinder teachers, I felt more able to ask for help, and was supported to have a better understanding of what I needed to do when I got home, so homework became far less stressful and anxiety inducing.

I think, looking back to my teens, I completely lost my identity. I did not know who I was. Like many girls with ADHD, I would flit around like a social butterfly, able to mask and appear to fit in, but never really feeling like I did.

I grade my older teen years as a C+.

I did okay in my GCSEs, certainly better than I would have done if I had stayed at my old secondary school, achieving mostly B's (with a sprinkling of A's and C's). Of course, I compared my results with the rest of my class, though, and felt I didn't measure up to them. I wish I had been told "Comparison is the thief of joy" (now one of my favourite quotes) when I was a child. Spending my life comparing myself to others who I perceived as "better than me" always

CHILDHOOD AND EDUCATION

made me feel that I was worth less than them. If I could go back and speak to myself as a child, I would say that I was kind, caring, funny and fun to be around. I would tell myself that I was more than "good enough".

This is why better understanding of ADHD in girls and women is so important, so that the generations of girls behind us won't grow up to become women who doubt themselves and wonder if they are good enough too.

> "When I hit my final year at school, though, I couldn't wait to leave. I spent the whole last year with my Walkman [a portable audio player] on and headphones in, listening to rock music, reinvented myself with Doc Martens boots, lots of black and a fake nose ring, and not really engaging with any of my peers. I spent the whole of my childhood feeling like I was more grown-up than my age, and I felt like I had outgrown school and the people there and couldn't wait for a new start."

COURTNEY

There is no doubt about it: our childhood experiences shape the adults we grow up to become.

I can see, looking back, that the crippling RSD and imposter syndrome that would go on to shape my adulthood began in my childhood because my ADHD was not diagnosed, and I just always felt a bit "different" to the other people around me.

Receiving my ADHD diagnosis has helped me move on from some of the trauma that I experienced in my younger years, and I no longer look back feeling shame and embarrassment, but rather pride at the strength I must have possessed to navigate such difficult times and come out as the woman I am now. I hope you can do the same.

(I thought you may also want to know that about ten years after I had left that secondary school that was hellish for me, when I was in my early twenties and had discovered Frizz Ease hair serum and mastered contact lenses, I bumped into Kevin in a local pub. As I stood at the bar, waiting to be served, a slightly paunchy man, wearing aftershave that was too strong, sidled up to me. As part of his very poor chat-up routine, he asked me my name. Fuelled by cheap white wine, I responded that I was surprised he didn't know my name as we had gone to school together, and that I knew his name was Kevin. He expressed genuine shock that we had gone to the same school, and replied, "I think I would have remembered if I had gone to school with you!" and then added, "You probably fancied me when you were there." To which I replied, "No, not really, and not nearly as much as you fancied yourself." I walked away from the bar and went to join my friends.)

WHAT ELSE COULD HELP?

As this chapter is about our childhoods, I have not included as much guidance and signposting here as I have in the other chapters – although our childhoods shape us, they cannot be changed. It may be painful and difficult to revisit your childhood, but it could also be an essential process for you to go through to realize that the challenges you experienced were not unique to you, and certainly not your fault.

- ✓ A neuro-affirming therapist or psychotherapist who really understands ADHD may be a useful person for you to discuss your childhood and related experiences and trauma with. Discussing how these have had an impact on and shaped you, and looking at how these can be turned into positives, can be incredibly powerful in your ADHD acceptance journey.
- ✓ Connecting with other women with ADHD through social media groups can be used in helping you realize that you are not alone in your experiences, which can also be very powerful.

Chapter Two

Parenting

(Some of you reading this book may not be parents. Perhaps you are not parents yet, perhaps you are not parents by choice, or perhaps this choice was made for you. If this chapter is not for you, then please feel free to skip it.)

Growing up, my interests would change regularly, as they do with ADHD. I would become obsessively interested in something, insist that my parents signed me up to a club or bought me something I needed, hyperfocus on it for a short while, only to lose interest very quickly. My ideas of what I wanted to do for a career and what my future would look like would change regularly and rapidly, often influenced by what my friends wanted to do or be.

But the one thing I never lost focus on and knew I wanted to be was…a mum.

At the time of writing this, it is over three years since my ADHD diagnosis, and still I have moments of clarity about how having ADHD has affected my life that are so incredibly obvious they almost stop me in my tracks. This is especially true when I consider how the impact of my undiagnosed ADHD has shaped my parenting.

As a child, I would regularly lose, break or get bored of my things. Like many children with ADHD, I was described as impatient, clumsy and careless on many occasions.

I remember once, as a teenager, becoming obsessed about getting a pair of Chelsea boots. I badgered my mum for weeks and did odd chores around the house until I finally had enough money to go into town and purchase a pair. When I got home, I tried my beautiful new boots on with various outfits. In between outfit changes, I was too impatient to bend down and remove my boots using my hands (the obvious choice), so I pulled one boot off with the other – and scraped all the leather on the front of one of my boots. I was mortified. My mum was really angry and made a comment that she wasn't surprised and that I was incapable of looking after my things.

Before I had my children, I got my first puppy. Bertie was a gorgeous little Border Terrier whom I adored. I had visions of him obediently following me around while I attended my horses, and so, when I had had him only a few weeks, I took him with me to the stables. As I led my horse in from her field, Bertie excitedly following me, I had a moment of happiness that my dream was happening – only to be halted by the worst noise I had ever heard as Bertie ran under my horse who, of course, stood on his paw. I was inconsolable and had to call my mum to come and take us both to the vets. As I explained to the vet what had happened, she told me that Bertie was clearly far too young to be let loose in a field, and that I was very fortunate that he was not more badly hurt. (He had some broken bones in his tiny little paw and had to rest for weeks, which blew out my plans of puppy training classes and lovely walks with my new friend.)

I left the vets feeling like the worst dog owner in the world, but also with the sense of utter failure that of course this had happened because I was clearly not capable of owning anything without it coming to some sort of harm or being damaged in some way.

When I had my children, I was utterly terrified of repeating my mistakes with so many other things that I valued and loved. I had this horrible sense of foreboding **all** the time that I was going to do something wrong, that my clumsiness, carelessness and forgetfulness (which were actually my undiagnosed ADHD symptoms) were going to lead to my beautiful babies being harmed, or worse. Looking back, I can now see that I had postnatal depression, but I masked it as I was so concerned that people would see that I was not able to look after my children properly and see me as an unfit mother. It would seem that many women with ADHD experience the same fears.

Research has shown that women with ADHD may experience more severe postnatal depression symptoms, and an increase in their ADHD symptoms, after giving birth. As women with ADHD, we are already experiencing RSD and imposter syndrome, and these compound our fears that we are "failing" at motherhood; the negative thinking patterns related to these can only increase our risk factor of experiencing postnatal depression.

> Research by J.J. Sandra Kooij in 2019 found that women with ADHD are more likely to experience hormone-related mood disorders, including postnatal depression. The study also showed that women who have ADHD experience more severe symptoms of conditions like postnatal depression than women without. In this study, 209 women aged from 18 to 71 with a diagnosis of ADHD seen in an outpatient clinic for adult ADHD were screened for various hormonal-related issues, including postnatal depression. The research showed that in the group of women who had at least one child, more than 57% had an EPDS (Edinburgh Postnatal Depression Scale) score of 10 or greater, meaning that they had (at least) mild postnatal depression. This percentage is significantly higher than the general population, where only 15% and 20% had an EPDS score of 10 or more.

A study by Anneli Andersson *et al.* in March 2023 concluded: "ADHD is an important risk factor for both depression and anxiety disorders postpartum. Therefore, ADHD needs to be considered in the maternal care, regardless of sociodemographic factors and the presence of other psychiatric disorders" (p.822).

"There were quite a few things that I never really understood at the time, but only now make perfect sense. I remember having a real epiphany moment reading an article on how postnatal depression doesn't look like someone just crying all the time – instead, it can manifest in getting angry really quickly. I wouldn't get sad or upset when overwhelmed; I'd be really pissed off and I would feel suffocated. The constant demands, the relentless touching, my brain was at capacity constantly."

IRIS

Some women have reported that their ADHD symptoms were not as bad during their pregnancy, and, again, this may be linked to hormones. During pregnancy, our bodies produce more oestrogen, and oestrogen is known to help with good brain functioning as it increases the body's production of dopamine and serotonin – our "happy hormones".

"I suffered with extreme prenatal and postnatal anxiety and depression after having both my children. The anxiety, imposter syndrome and rejection sensitive dysphoria I experienced caused me to question everything I was doing as a mother. Was I a good mum? Do they love me? Will this cause them trauma later in life? I felt like I had failed them if I did something even slightly wrong. My thoughts would go round and round with constant worries day and night. And yet I masked so much to appear like everything was wonderful, keeping everything hidden."

LAUREN

"I believe I had undiagnosed postnatal depression, which was slightly different for each child. First time round I had to do everything as 'perfectly' and routinely as I possibly could. I worried about all the milestones. With my second child, I left him at home with his dad when he was six weeks old and returned to work, as I could not cope."

CARLEIGH

In addition to our hormones raging and fluctuating, our lives are turned upside down with the arrival of our

PARENTING

long-awaited bundles of joy. We become sleep-deprived, and any semblance of order that we have, managed to force into our lives, despite our ADHD, gets dismantled before our barely open eyes – as if sleep wasn't a big enough challenge for us as women with ADHD already?!

I experienced horrible anxiety as a new mum, and a lot of this was due to imposter syndrome.

Imposter syndrome causes feelings of incompetency and unworthiness. Even with the evidence screaming and pooing in my hands, I still felt like a fraud. I constantly compared myself and my parenting to others. If I went to a mother and toddler group and was asked questions like, "Is he sleeping through the night yet?" I felt like a failure as my mothering never seemed to be on a par with others.

As a new parent, I felt I always **had** to do the right thing, and this put me under enormous pressure to be "perfect". I also don't think it helped that I had my first baby when Gina "**effing**" Ford was all the rage! So, pressure to literally do everything "by the book", which is so hard to do when you have ADHD, set me up to fail.

I wish I could go back in time and do it "my way" without all the real and perceived expectations I placed on myself. As women with ADHD, the pressure we put on ourselves can really spoil the things we should be able to enjoy.

"I always felt messy, disorganized, exhausted and lazy, but I got by with lists and strategies in place. Then my wife had our twins when I was 35. She had undiagnosed postnatal depression and I became the main earner in our family, but I found the sleep deprivation, the constant demand, the monotony of feeds and naps and nappy changes as well as working full time so hard. I survived on can after can of Diet Coke to get me through each day."

COURTNEY

"Before I had a child, I hadn't really had to run a house or really had any sort of routine…although I was desperate to be a mother. My anxiety kicked in during labour and continued. I love being a mum and love kids. Exploring the world with my son has been one of the biggest joys of my life, but I always felt I needed more children to be a real family. I felt this sense of guilt that I hadn't provided siblings. This made us not quite normal, but I have never felt normal, so why start now? I think subconsciously I knew that I wouldn't cope with having another child."

ANDREA

PARENTING

Now, I expect most new parents experience some level of imposter syndrome. We are constantly bombarded with images of "perfect parents" through the media – celebrities who have seemingly snapped back into shape, models having their makeup done while breastfeeding their beautiful babies, and even nappy adverts of slim, showered and dressed new mums rolling around on perfectly made white linen beds. These images make us think that this is what parenting will be like, and should be like. In reality, I was a mess, my house was a mess, and the only shit I could get together some days was bundled up in a nappy.

When you have ADHD, your executive functioning means that it can be a daily struggle to plan and organize yourself, so the treadmill of life that involves running a home, planning meals, remembering appointments, personal hygiene, time management, getting washing done, paying the bills on time, etc., which is already hard enough to manage when you have ADHD, gets even harder when you become a new parent.

When your hormones are raging and you are sleep-deprived, your already impaired executive functioning may as well get in the nappy bin among the ever-growing pile of nappies, because you keep forgetting to empty it!

> "I remember realizing that it never stops, there are no breaks – once you're a mother, you're always a mother. Now, looking back, I realize how I used to use my alone time to decompress from all the socializing life brings. However, the structure of having a child was good for me. When my two boys were in full-time school, that's when I started to fall apart and realize that I struggled with days with no structure. I found the days I worked were easier than the days when I was off."

SARAH M

I hid it well and masked all my insecurities, but in reality, I felt like a fraud and, at times, a failure. I didn't want people to know the truth about my struggles. As a new parent, I got out of bed, already exhausted most mornings, and donned my mask of the "perfect mum".

Whether it is to try to fit in or hide our self-identified inadequacies, the need to mask our way through parenting is something that so many of us with ADHD have felt we have had to do.

Masking in itself is exhausting, so I set up a really negative cycle, as the more tired I was, the worse my executive functioning became, and the harder I tried to hide the impacts of this, the more I masked. I was scared to admit how much I was struggling or to ask for help, as

PARENTING

I worried that others would also see me as the failure I felt I was.

The constant comparison in my mind of what I should be like as a parent just made my imposter syndrome soar.

> "When I struggled with tasks, I would berate myself endlessly and wonder why I couldn't cope like everyone else and found it so hard. In fact, to my surprise, most people seemed to think I was so organized. My constant need to make people like me and see me as the perfect, got-it-all-together mum meant that I became so anxious about forgetting anything. Looking back now, I realize I'd found my own ways to manage, but it was utterly exhausting. I'd labelled myself as lazy and a bad mum, and felt so much shame around this."

AMY

My imposter syndrome was so bad I even felt like a fraud watching *Milkshake* on TV in the early hours. When I saw all those perfect mums sending in birthday cards for their children's first and second birthdays, it made me feel like a failure because I never did it, which is quite frankly ridiculous, as what one- or two-year-old would appreciate or remember this gesture of perfect motherly love?!

> "Being really sound sensitive, it was very hard not to feel triggered by crying and noise in general, even though I'm noisy myself! I found it difficult to moderate my emotions around this. To be honest, this brought lots of shame and imposter syndrome – am I really capable of doing this? Does everyone feel this way?"

KELLY

I did meet some friends through mother and baby and toddler groups when my eldest was young. But again, I always felt like I didn't really fit, and I used to get terrible social anxiety about going. I think I would have been much happier just staying at home with my children and playing in the garden with our dog, but again, I succumbed to the expectation that I **should** be attending these groups.

I found these groups very cliquey, and, of course, my eldest son, James, who was later diagnosed with ADHD, was not the type of child to sit quietly and play or join in the songs at the end, so I often left feeling judged and worse than I did when I arrived. My imposter syndrome kicked in again at these meet-ups, because, in my eyes, everyone else just seemed to be doing so much better than I was.

Sometimes, I would actually "pull a sicky" to avoid going to the groups, because I didn't want to admit to anyone that I wasn't really enjoying them, and that I would be looked on as a "bad parent" if I wasn't taking my children along to

PARENTING

interact with others, sing "Wind the Bobbin Up" and play with the germ-smeared group toys, which then led to some genuine, and at times much appreciated, reasons not to go!

> "When I had my first and second child, I wanted to make friends with other mums locally. I regularly attended many mother and baby groups; however, I never made a close friend from them. I always felt I was very different to the other mums but did not know why. It was like I could not connect with them and only on a superficial level. It was not until my diagnosis that I understood."

HAZEL-LEE

As they got older, I became fiercely protective of my children. I wanted to prove to everyone that I **could** care for things and look after them. I wanted everyone to see that I **was** the "perfect mum".

If anyone dared criticize my parenting or my children, it would illicit the most visceral and powerful emotional response in me. I would cut myself off from friends who told me my whirlwind of a toddler James needed more boundaries. I once had a huge row with one of his teachers who complained about his "forgetfulness" and "disorganization" in the least sympathetic and most unhelpful way I had ever heard a teacher talk about a child.

But then the RSD that is also associated with ADHD kicked in, and I agonized about what they were saying about me in the staff room, and hated the fact that I was probably seen as "one of those parents" now.

> "I was always the mum who was crying at the school gates, worrying about my children not keeping up or something else. I was unable to control emotions and think clearly about the situation, which was a little thing but felt like a huge thing to me."
>
>

SARAH D

When James was in Year 4, I took him to the GP as I was becoming increasingly concerned about him and his behaviour. I was constantly being told by his school that he was unable to sit still, forgetful, distracting and distracted. James was referred to a paediatrician who was lovely and stated that she felt he was "ADD with a touch of H". The next stage of James's assessment was for the paediatrician to observe him at school and for the school to complete paperwork, including Conners Questionnaires.[1]

Unfortunately, when completing the paperwork, James's school completely downplayed all the difficulties James was experiencing, so the paediatrician was unable to give

---

[1] See, for example, www.verywellmind.com/the-conners-4-adhd-assessment-test-how-its-used-scoring-7104954

PARENTING

a diagnosis. He was finally diagnosed with "combined subtype" ADHD when he was in Year 8 at school, after a really difficult and challenging time, and one of my greatest regrets is not advocating harder for him when he was still in primary school. It seemed particularly ironic that during this time I was a head teacher at a specialist school and later became an ADHD trainer – things that only amplified my feelings of guilt that James was so misunderstood and unsupported for as long as he was in school.

> "Things got harder when they started school. I did more school pick-ups and drop-offs and they took so much out of me. They were always getting in trouble at school and I hated the judgement from teachers and other parents."

> COURTNEY

Why didn't I advocate harder, you ask? I believe there are a few reasons for this.

I think the way James behaved at school mirrored my own behaviour when I was younger. Because of this, I didn't really understand that it was "different" to how other children behaved, because, to me, it was "normal". When his teacher pointed out he had painted his shoes rather than his paper at school, I thought this was funny and showed his creativity (his teacher was clearly not in agreement with this!), but this was the sort of thing I would have done when I was a child. I am not alone in my feelings that I could have advocated harder for the smallest and most important people in my life.

> "I didn't advocate near enough for my first daughter as I have done for my second daughter. Through fear of being judged and being that parent! I wanted people to like me. And it didn't necessarily matter who it was. Other parents, teachers, the kids' friends and so on, I wanted them to perceive me as a kind, nice person, without rocking the boat."
>
>

KATE

We know that ADHD runs in families, and I have identified many members of my family who I believe are undiagnosed ADHD. When James received his diagnosis at the age of 12, the paediatrician explained that it ran in families and said to James's dad and me, "One of you is very likely to also have ADHD." James's dad turned to me and said, "Well, that will be you!" But even with my experiences of working with students with ADHD, the penny didn't quite drop. Perhaps I wasn't ready to accept the diagnosis at that stage, or perhaps I was just more focused on the "textbook" understanding and medical model of ADHD that I still held on to at that time. Like so many other women with ADHD, my own child's diagnosis led me to getting my own.

PARENTING

"Like many others before me, I only considered my own ADHD when my child was referred for assessment. I had the usual stereotype of delinquent boys so I Googled ADHD in girls... Three hours later, I put down my phone to try and sleep, cheeks wet from crying. So, just maybe, I wasn't a sh*t human being after all . Maybe there was a reason for being and finding things difficult."

DEBORAH

We have seen an increase in adult diagnoses of autism and ADHD in recent years, but there are many people who still don't "get" ADHD. How many times have you heard or read comments such as "We didn't have all these conditions in my day?" Oh yes, we did!!!! We just saw them as negative behaviours, such as laziness, naughtiness, being disorganized, etc.

I think it can be hard for family members to accept that ADHD is actually "a thing" because they are ignorant of the facts, but because it also shines a light on the challenges they have experienced, and the stigma that is sadly still attached to ADHD means this can be hard to accept.

I hope, so much, that future generations have a better understanding of neurodiversity, because understanding your neurotype and how it impacts on your life can be an absolute game-changer when it comes to self-acceptance and positive mental health.

> "Being a mum to two neurodivergent children, I started to look at my own life a lot closer. Being their biggest fan and their strongest advocate led me to a string of lightbulb moments about my own life and, perhaps arguably, my own sense of wellbeing and mental health. I was awoken to the fact that I could speak very honestly for them because of my own lived experience and my huge empathy and sensitivity to the world around me...and that, actually, I could finally see this as my gift and something to celebrate!"

BETHANY

To get back on track, I am a "people pleaser", and like many others I know with ADHD, I am afraid of confrontation. My fear of upsetting James's school and being seen as "one of those parents" stopped me from challenging things that instinctively did not feel right.

I always tell parents to trust their gut and follow their instincts, as mine were never wrong when it came to what my children needed.

Despite the fact I worked in education, I didn't really understand what James was entitled to in a mainstream school without a diagnosis. If I had armed myself with more information and facts, I would have felt better equipped to fight harder for him.

PARENTING

My experiences as a parent have really shaped the work I do as a professional working with neurodivergent parents of neurodivergent children.

I absolutely hate seeing parents of neurodivergent children as "overly anxious" or "overprotective".

I hate it when parents' views on their children are disregarded by so-called experts. I know that actually parents are the experts on their children and **must** be listened to and believed, and I always remember this when I am working with parents in any form.

I am not a boastful person, but I do know that I like the parents I work with who are also ADHD, and I am a bloody good mum. I just wish that I had understood myself and my brain and known about my ADHD when I was younger.

Because if I had known when I was younger that I had ADHD when I was younger, I would have masked less, advocated harder and been far, far kinder to myself. I would have been able to tell myself that my brain was telling me that I was a fraud or an imposter, and that it was lying to me.

I would have told myself that I wasn't lazy or a walking disaster, because I would have understood the impact of my raging hormones on my already impaired executive functioning.

I would not have subjected myself to social situations that

actually left me feeling drained and even more tired than I already was. I would be content being authentically me, and I would recognize how brilliantly I was actually doing. I would tell myself that parenting is, at times, bloody hard work, and that as women with ADHD, it is okay to struggle and not be perfect all the time. Remember, sometimes you can only do your "best", and your "best" will change each day, but your best is also always good enough.

> "I want others to know they aren't alone and they're not 'doing it wrong'. I'm autistic and ADHD, and before I had a child, I managed pretty well on a surface level. I'd built a life that accommodated my needs as much as possible. With a child in the mix, it's too much. I want others to know that it's okay to ask or pay for help. Now I know why I have issues with executive functioning, I don't feel guilty about things like hiring a cleaner."

LIZZIE

Looking back, I can also see that there are elements of my ADHD that make me a really good mum! There was a lot of joy and laughter in my home when my kids were young. I know that I was good fun, spontaneous, adventurous and creative – all the positive attributes of ADHD that should not be hidden away but celebrated. My kids didn't care that the house was a mess and at times resembled the aftermath of a bomb going off in Toys "R" Us; they didn't care that the washing-up got left for days or that their clothes weren't ironed, because I know they always felt a lot of love, and that is reflected in the brilliant relationships we have now.

WHAT ELSE COULD HELP?

- ✓ Tune in to your negative thoughts about your parenting. It can be helpful to write things down, putting them in black and white. Then challenge your thinking. For example, "I am a terrible parent, I am so forgetful and my house is a mess!" Instead, you should think, "My house isn't the tidiest, but that is because I spend my time playing with my kids instead of cleaning, which they will appreciate far more!" Focus on what goes well, not what doesn't.
- ✓ Ask for support if you need it. It doesn't make you a bad parent or a failure to admit that you are struggling. People don't offer if they think you are coping, and no one will think less of you if you admit you are in need of some help.
- ✓ Focus on the things that bring you and your children happiness, and avoid the pressure to conform with what others do.
- ✓ Don't be scared to say "no". You don't have to accept every invite, go to every party or social event with your child. You don't have to commit to every opportunity to help at the school. Be firm, but fair, and just explain that you don't have time to commit

to anything extra at the moment, but that you appreciate being asked.
- ✓ Follow your instincts and trust your gut. Your instincts as a parent are unlikely to be wrong.
- ✓ Educate yourself on your child's rights. Arm yourself with the facts about what your child is entitled to, and remember that facts are worth more than opinions. When having meetings or communication with professionals about your child, try to keep emotions at bay. Re-read emails before you send them to remove emotional statements, or ask a trusted friend to read them through for you before you press send. If you feel angry or upset about something in relation to your child, wait before you email or speak to someone, and communicate when you feel calmer.
- ✓ Become your child's advocate – remember that **you** are the expert on your child. Remind yourself that you know your child better than any other person, and don't be scared to become "that parent". Your teacher will only be in your child's life for an academic year or two, but you will be their parent all their life.
- ✓ Remember, "Comparison is the thief of joy". There is no such thing as the "perfect" parent or family. Comparing yourself to others and what you perceive their family or parenting is like, particularly when confronted with images on social media, will potentially increase feelings of negativity and failure.

PARENTING

Useful links

Postnatal support

APNI (Association for Post Natal Illness) was established in 1979 to provide support to anyone suffering from or affected by postnatal illness, including partners, family and friends, to increase public awareness of the illness and to encourage research into its cause/nature: https://apni.org

Maternal Mental Health Alliance is a network of 130 organizations, dedicated to ensuring women and families affected by perinatal mental health problems have access to high-quality, compassionate care: https://maternalmentalhealthalliance.org

PANDAS (PND Awareness and Support) offers hope, empathy and support for every parent or network affected by perinatal mental illness: www.pandasfoundation.org.uk

Support and advocacy for neurodivergent children

IPSEA (Independent Provider of Special Education Advice) provides free and independent legal advice and support to families of children and young people with SEND: www.ipsea.org.uk

SOS!SEN helps families secure the right special educational

provision for children and young people with SEND: https://sossen.org.uk

Special Needs Jungle is for those who do not know where to look or how to cut their way through the increasingly complicated SEND system; this organization aims to highlight and provide resources and inspire and empower families: www.specialneedsjungle.com

Chapter Three

ADHD, Hormones and Menopause

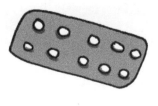

Like so many other neurodivergent women, I have always had some dodgy stuff going on with my hormones. Although there is already plenty of evidence that oestrogen impacts our mood and behaviour, and there are plenty of neurotypical women who suffer with their hormones, researchers are only now really starting to understand the link between hormones and ADHD. The hormonal changes we experience that start in puberty and continue throughout adulthood seem to really have an impact on women with ADHD.

> "I have some of the features of high testosterone – increased muscle mass, acne, small breasts. I have a prolactinoma, which caused high prolactin, which, in turn, affected my reproductive hormones. I believe I have high cortisol, quite possibly (in part) due to being ND [neurodivergent] in a NT [neurotypical] world, and I have always had an irregular cycle compared to what is considered 'normal'."

SARAH B

It would appear, however, that ADHD can really amplify hormone-related issues, and as a result, many women with ADHD struggle even more than their neurotypical peers with many of the wonderful things we have to endure as women.

> "I've always struggled with PMT [premenstrual tension] and hormones. Everything around the time of the month becomes so incredibly heightened; I can't bear to be touched, noise sensitivity goes through the roof, and generally I become very snappy and moody. Sudden loud noises make me shout. My concentration is also affected as I find I become less motivated and procrastinate a lot more during hormonal periods."

MADDIE

I was quite late to start my periods, but before I did so, I used to get a horrific migraine every four weeks or so. I hated having periods so much. I found them hell from a sensory perspective, and also extremely inconvenient! I was also paranoid about "leaking", and often did not want to leave the house when I had my period in case this happened. I also spent a lot of time in a leotard as a teenager doing gymnastics, an item of clothing not designed to be worn with bulky sanitary products!!

My periods were never really regular, and it took me over two years to get pregnant with my first son. Having an irregular cycle when you are desperate for a baby is hard. Lots of my friends were getting pregnant really easily, and outwardly I would be happy for them, while inside I was screaming with jealousy.

I would be late for my period and would try not to get too excited, knowing that it would probably be like every other month, but my impatience would take over and I would buy a pregnancy test, only for it to be negative...again. I spent a bloody fortune on pregnancy tests and a lot of time crying in my bathroom. Mother Nature is a right bitch sometimes.

Eventually, I went to my GP and was referred for tests. These showed that I had polycystic ovary syndrome (PCOS) and a severely underactive thyroid. It was no wonder I couldn't get pregnant.

> A study in 2015 by Sabri Hergüner *et al.*, titled, "Attention deficit-hyperactivity disorder symptoms in women with polycystic ovary syndrome", concluded that "women with PCOS have higher ADHD symptoms" (p.2).

This is again something I wish I had been aware of back in my twenties, as it may have encouraged me to seek a diagnosis far, far sooner.

> Another common gynaecological problem that many women with ADHD experience is endometriosis. A study by Terri D'Arrigo in 2020 found that women with a diagnosis of endometriosis had higher rates of a range of mental health conditions, including ADHD, than women who did not have endometriosis.

This, again, raises the question of why medical professionals are not joining the dots around neurodivergent women and hormonal issues when so many of us are suffering so much.

It took me two years to finally conceive my eldest son. My second son was conceived far quicker, and I think perhaps my first pregnancy kicked my body into action, and, of course, my thyroid was sorted out by then too.

After having my children, my periods still never returned

to a regular cycle, and I actually **hated** having periods still. They were still extremely messy and inconvenient – not because I was still wearing leotards (I wasn't), but they just got in the way and meant there was an extra level of organization required in my life to always ensure I had sanitary products and remembered to change my tampon. (Who else was terrified at the prospect of catching toxic shock syndrome, which sounds like an evil character from *The Incredibles*!)

> "Puberty was particularly difficult, made even harder by the fact that I had undiagnosed endometriosis for many years. While the oestrogen from my HRT [hormone replacement therapy] keeps my brain stable, it does, unfortunately, continue to feed my endometriosis, but I would take stable mind over stable body every time."

JODY

Having a coil fitted was a way I could abolish periods from my life, but was yet another painful and awkward experience I endured as a woman.

I once had a coil changed and refitted by a slightly terrifying Russian doctor. As I lay on the narrow bed with my legs spread apart, she asked me, "You have taken painkillers?" "Err… No?!" I replied anxiously, to which she replied, "Ah, you think you are brave, huh?" I certainly felt less brave after that exchange!

On a more recent coil change experience, the lovely lady GP was clearly trying to distract me and make me feel more comfortable and asked me what I did for a job. When I told her what I did, she said, "Oh, you're Laura Kerbey, the autism lady! I thought I recognized your name!" She then told me she had an autistic son and we started to have a really long chat about neurodiversity and the state of the education and healthcare system for neurodivergent children.

All the time I was lying there, naked from the waist down, legs spread again, while she poked and prodded. I offered to bring some flyers into the surgery, and we agreed to go for a coffee before she asked me to put my knickers back on and reminded me that she had other patients waiting. (I haven't met her for coffee; I feel a bit weird about it now she has seen me without my knickers on!)

The coil doesn't work for everyone, but it definitely worked for me. I didn't have a period for years, thank God, and just kind of forgot about them. So the next time I really became aware of the impact of hormones was about two years ago, when I was 48.

I met up with one of my best friends, Andrea, who is also diagnosed with ADHD, and as we sat in the sunshine, I told her how much I was struggling. I told her:

"My memory is terrible."
"I'm not sleeping well."
"My anxiety is so high."
"My executive functioning is terrible."

I told her that my ADHD felt like it was getting worse and was off the scale! I told her that I had been dropping the ball a lot recently and that that was making me super-anxious. The more anxious I got, the worse my executive functioning was becoming, and I seemed trapped in this horrible cycle.

Andrea told me, "Laura, speak to your doctor! Your ADHD is not getting worse; you are probably perimenopausal!" The idea had not actually occurred to me as I thought menopause was something that happened to "older ladies", and I definitely didn't feel like an "older lady" yet.

Those of us with ADHD can find that our symptoms get worse as we approach menopause.

> "I have now been in perimenopause for five years. The biggest impact it has had is on my working memory. It is the worst my ADHD has been. I can't remember the word I need to say, people's names, even what they look like sometimes. My attention span is the worst it's ever been, and I have bursts of energy, but otherwise I feel tired most of the time."

JAYNE

For many years, medical professionals have understood that there is a link between menopause and oestrogen, and that as you approach perimenopause, your oestrogen levels begin to drop by as much as 65%. When oestrogen levels decrease, your cognitive ability will drop too, which results in memory and processing difficulties and brain fog. A reduction in oestrogen may also cause mood disorders.

> "It certainly feels like there has been a change in my hormones as I approach menopause that has compounded my ADHD 'symptoms'. Combined with the accumulative exhaustion of masking my way through life, the burnout I have hit in recent years is like I've not experienced before. My physical and mental health is at an all-time low, and my ability to cope with my ADHD and autistic differences has reduced dramatically."
>
> RACHAEL

> "It is my intellectual and educated understanding that dopamine and oestrogen are inextricably linked; it is my lived experience that they are brutally entangled. I am officially in menopause and ecstatic about it too; it marks the end of a life dominated by hormones and the end to a rollercoaster ride I never asked to be on."

JODY

It is not just oestrogen levels that fall during menopause. Menopause also affects levels of dopamine because oestrogen regulates the functioning of dopamine and, of course, dopamine is something we are already lacking and plays a central role in ADHD and executive functioning.

Our serotonin levels, which are needed for the regulation of mood and noradrenaline levels, also drop during this time.

I mean, come on, Mother Nature, this is all stuff we are struggling with anyway – why do you have to make it even harder for us?! (I swear she must be neurotypical!!)

> "I am bang in the middle of menopause and I have found this the most confidence-sapping aspect of my hormones affecting my ADHD (and vice versa). There are so many overlaps, such as brain fog, forgetfulness, leading to a loss of confidence, or feeling a bit useless. Also loads of stomach problems as a result of ADHD, but worsened by the menopause."

KATIE

It is also worth noting that ADHD medication may not work as well when your oestrogen levels are lower, so during your period and when you become perimenopausal. This would also be something to discuss with your psychiatrist or GP. On the flip side, HRT can increase the effectiveness of ADHD meds.

After my time with Andrea, I did make an appointment to see the GP, and I was really lucky because she was amazing – she seemed to really understand my symptoms and the fact that my ADHD was exacerbating them.

We came up with a plan together, and two years on, I am on HRT, which has really helped me. The only thing I struggle with now is remembering to take the bloody stuff!

> "Knowing my ADHD has made me more aware and in tune with my feelings and emotions. I definitely can feel the hormonal changes each month much more exaggerated now. I feel like I am a work in progress during these times of the month. Like I am mentoring myself from the outside to guide myself through it, in a neurodivergently affirmative way."

MICHELE

I know I was really lucky with that GP, because I saw someone who really understood the impact that menopause can have on ADHD; sadly, I also know that lots of other women with ADHD have not been so lucky. One lady I know went to see her GP about her perimenopausal challenges and her (male) GP said patronizingly, "Oh, another one who has watched that Davina McCall programme!" (Do not get me started on how different the world would be if men went through "The Change"!)

Something that I feel blessed not to experience, but that I know is a real challenge for many women with ADHD, is premenstrual dysphoric disorder (PMDD). PMDD is like PMS, but much, much worse. Symptoms of PMDD can include:

- Low mood and feeling overwhelmed and helpless
- High anxiety
- Irritability and extreme mood changes
- Extreme tiredness and fatigue
- Overeating and excessive food cravings
- Bloating, breast tenderness and weight gain
- Headaches, muscle and joint pain
- Increased aggression towards self and others
- Suicidal ideation or attempts.

> "I was diagnosed with PMDD years ago. I was an absolute nightmare and couldn't hold a relationship down. The two weeks before my period was due, I was an argumentative dickhead; once my period started, I was back to what I preferred as my 'normal' self."
>
> **DEBBIE M**

> PMDD can be really serious if not properly understood and treated. A study by Divya Prasad *et al.*, published in the *Journal of Women's Health* in 2021, found that adults with PMDD are seven times more likely to die by suicide than adults without premenstrual disorders.

> A further study by Farangis Dorani *et al.* in 2021 concluded that 45.5% of women with ADHD experience PMDD compared with a reported 28.7% in the general population.

"I can remember having difficulty with PMDD before, when I was younger, but I could manage my behaviour when I needed to, like when I worked with children in a primary school. As I get older, I have noticed that PMDD has become more intense for me, and little things can shift my mood quickly. I can get very sensitive and defensive to real or perceived criticism, I can be argumentative, and I have had a few rage-y meltdowns during these hormonal shifts. I have had to apologize to my spouse many times for this, and I have to remind myself to keep track of my cycle, so I know when my 'crazy time' is coming."

STEPHANIE

PMDD is yet another area that seems to be widely misunderstood and in greater need of far more research, understanding and support.

I hope, so much, that the medical profession begins to understand the utterly debilitating impact hormones can have on women in general and, in particular, those of us who are neurodivergent, who seem to suffer more than most.

> **WHAT ELSE COULD HELP?**
>
> ✓ First, if you feel that you are struggling with hormonal issues, do speak to your GP. Don't suffer in silence! If you are not happy with your GP's response, ask to see another doctor.
> ✓ Increase your protein intake as protein can help with hormones by providing amino acids, which are needed for hormone production.
> ✓ Increase your healthy fat intake (in moderation – yes, I know this is hard!).
> ✓ Increase your calcium intake to reduce the risk of osteoporosis.
> ✓ Reduce your caffeine and sugar intake (yes, I know this is hard too!).
> ✓ Try to increase the amount of exercise you do.
>
> (A lot of the recommendations in Chapter Six, such as reducing stress and getting good sleep, are also

really important considerations when you are peri/menopausal too.)

Useful links

Menopause

Menopause Support provides private support via telephone and video consultations, and bespoke menopause training and support solutions for businesses and organizations, as well as menopause training days for therapists and wellbeing professionals: https://menopausesupport.co.uk

The Menopause Charity aims to educate everybody so that perimenopause and menopause are properly understood: www.themenopausecharity.org

Endometriosis

Endometriosis UK, the UK's leading charity for all those affected by endometriosis, is determined to ensure that everyone gets prompt diagnosis and the best treatment and support: www.endometriosis-uk.org

PMDD

IAPMD (International Association for Post Menstrual Disorders) provides a lifeline of support, information and resources for women and AFAB (assigned female at birth) individuals with PMDD and premenstrual exacerbation (PME): https://iapmd.org

Chapter Four

Rejection Sensitive Dysphoria and Imposter Syndrome

Rejection sensitive dysphoria

When I was finally diagnosed with ADHD, I don't think anyone who knew me well was surprised! I started to research ADHD more and had my biggest "lightbulb" moment when reading about rejection sensitive dysphoria (RSD). Again, I am not alone in feeling this way.

> "I think reading about **RSD** and imposter syndrome were the biggest lightbulb moments in my ADHD journey so far."
>
>
>
> LUCY

Although RSD is not just experienced by people with ADHD, some studies report that 98% of us with ADHD experience it. Symptoms include:

- Being overly sensitive to criticism
- Being sensitive to disapproval from others
- Having raised anxiety
- People pleasing, fawning and approval-seeking behaviour
- Experiencing low self-esteem and low self-worth
- Avoiding social situations
- Fear of failure and self-sabotaging behaviours
- Setting unrealistic expectations for oneself
- Experiencing strong emotional outbursts after being hurt or feeling rejected.

In basic terms, experiencing RSD means that you experience extremely strong emotions, or even pain, at real or perceived feelings of rejection. RSD can impact our mental health, our relationships, friendships and careers. It can be quite debilitating for those of us who have ADHD.

Remember in Chapter One I mentioned that statistic that children with ADHD receive 20,000 more negative comments by the age of 12 than their neurodivergent peers? Well, imagine how many negative comments we have received by the time we are in adulthood!

> "Nobody likes rejection, but RSD can be debilitating and last for years. I think for me RSD really comes into play when I re-live things that have gone on in my past that were what a lot of people would call minor incidents. Like the time I pulled out in front of a car, and they beeped me – that was probably 20 years ago now, yet I still have moments of shame as I recall that time. I would run the scene over and over in my head, feeling awful and believing that person must think I'm a horrible human being."
>
> **RSD**

AMY

I have always been described as "oversensitive" or as someone who would "overreact" to situations. If I was told off at school, reprimanded at work, criticized, even only slightly by a friend or partner, I would be completely devastated. I would spend hours ruminating over conversations or comments and read negativity into them, which would make me incredibly anxious.

On top of this, my go-to feeling when walking into a room of people would be "They won't like me", which would result in my trying way too hard to get them to like me. I would try super-hard to be funny, serious, intellectual, silly, flirty

– whatever I felt that person needed me to be – which is utterly exhausting, and also means that I rejected my own persona so much I often lost sight of who I truly was.

In my later teens and early adulthood, I started to feel so anxious about social situations that I would need to drink alcohol to become "fun, crazy Laura", as I felt that was who people expected me to be. I was given the nickname "Laura, You Can't Ignore 'Er" as I was always so loud and over the top at parties. That made me feel like I was "too much" and an attention seeker, when I actually often just wanted to remain invisible and unnoticed.

> "At school, and especially university, I was the life and soul, literally burning myself out going out partying every night, missing lectures, feeling the need to be busy all the time and not being able to say 'no'! I'm typically the last man standing, but very recently I'm trying to take better care of myself and being more self-aware and realizing when I need to stop and recharge. I have always suffered from major FOMO!! Escapism is a massive part of my life, whether it be through partying, drink, experimenting at university."
>
> RSD
>
> JAIME

After social situations, when I had been drinking, I would then have terrible mental hangovers when "the fear" of what I had done would give me absolutely terrible anxiety the next day, and after a night out I would replay every single conversation over and over again in my head, analyzing every comment I had made, and cringing at myself. This just fuelled the cycle of anxiety, as I would get so anxious about my next social encounter that I would repeat my actions over and over again.

> "Finding out about RSD was powerful. All my life I've been terrified of 'being in trouble' with people I love and like. I now realize that this fear is actually a fear of rejection. A text from a friend saying 'Call me now' injects my body with a whole shot of fear; rationality flies out. Even though I know I've done nothing to upset them, my assumption is that I must have done, and they are now furious and want me to call so they can confront me. I panic and have to stop whatever I am doing to immediately call them. Inevitably, they simply didn't want to ring as they thought I was busy, but had a question or something to say that they didn't want to forget. My body is then left processing the residual effects of the adrenaline." **RSD**

MEGAN

Criticism in any shape or form is almost painful for me to receive. It's not that I don't think I deserve criticism – I have lived all my life expecting it – but when people criticize me, it feels as though I've let them down, and then I have let myself down too.

I'm also a huge catastrophizer, so if people aren't happy with me, I get really paranoid about them telling other people I'm useless, that other people won't want to work with me, that my career is over and I need to become an Ocado driver! (Yes, I have actually thought that!)

> "When people don't reply to a text message or an email, I automatically default to the notion that I must have done something wrong in previous interactions or offended them somehow. Writing and sending emails is particularly hard, because I have to go over them so many times to ensure that every word is 'perfect' or accurate and that nothing can be misinterpreted. Sometimes I even send draft emails to friends to check how my tone reads, or if I could be interpreted discordantly with my intention." RSD
>
> SARAH B

A huge source of RSD for me is social media. Social media is a necessity for my work, but I find it incredibly anxiety-provoking at times. All it takes is one "angry face" reaction or someone disagreeing with me, and I feel my anxiety soar. I have been trolled on Facebook a few times, and it was awful. I honestly felt attacked and terrified and could not sleep on each occasion. I know people say to "just ignore the trolls" and that they are "keyboard warriors", but I can't help but take their comments to heart, and those comments are incredibly wounding.

So how do I support myself to deal with my RSD?

I blame my brain. I remind myself that there is a negative voice in my head trying to trick me into thinking that people don't like me, that I'm not good enough, and that I'm a fake.

I tell myself that my brain is lying to me because it's wired differently. My brain is receiving signals about people around me inaccurately, so I just need to retune the messages as I receive them.

When I come out of a meeting and cringe, thinking, "Laura, you weren't good enough in there" or "you weren't as good as the other professionals in there", I remind myself that these are lies – that they wouldn't have asked me to come back again if my input wasn't valuable.

> "Now knowing why this response is provoked means that I am better able to challenge the initial thoughts. It's still a work in progress, as I have decades of muscle and emotion memory to try and reprogramme, but I've started!"
>
> RSD

MEGAN

REJECTION SENSITIVE DYSPHORIA AND IMPOSTER SYNDROME

Someone gave me some amazing advice once; they told me to "take my thoughts to court" and to search for the evidence of whether my negative thoughts were real or false. It's hard to do it in the moment, but it can stop my ruminating negative thoughts, or "washing machine head", as I call it.

I can also remind myself that not everyone will like me, and that's okay! I don't like everyone - so why should everyone like me?!

I also talk about my feelings. I'm blessed to have amazing (mainly ND [neurodivergent]) friends who know I get really anxious about what people think, and know how to help me make sense of my thoughts and see what's real and what's not. They can help me find the evidence that disproves what my brain is telling me.

When I receive criticism, I try to "scale it down" and think, "Ouch! That hurt and felt like a 8/10 on the criticism scale - so it was probably only meant as about a 4/10."

If a friend does not respond to a text or call straight away, I try to tell myself that they are busy, or, as most of my good friends are also ADHD, that they have probably just read the message, got distracted and forgotten to reply. Sometimes, I may even message a friend and say something like, "All okay? Not heard back from you and the RSD is really RSDing!" and then I usually get a response back from them immediately, apologizing profusely.

My RSD and fear of people not liking me has led to me becoming a massive people pleaser. I can see that this is something that has been a part of me and impacted all my friendships and relationships most of my life. I have a fear of people not liking me, which has meant that I have put other people's happiness and needs above my own, often to my own detriment. Saying "no" to other people has been incredibly hard for me, and this has led to me being taken advantage of in many ways.

> "I 'fawn'. I'm a people pleaser. I put other people's needs and feelings above mine constantly. I push myself beyond my limits daily in an attempt to avoid criticism or rejection. This is an entirely maladaptive 'coping mechanism' because I have found myself in dangerous situations through fawning, and, of course, it is hugely exhausting." **RSD**

RACHAEL

My people pleasing is so extreme that despite being absolutely terrified of heights, I once jumped out of an aeroplane because I didn't want to let people down.

I was in my twenties and at the pub when a friend of a friend arrived. She was upset because she had arranged a group trip to do a parachute jump, and someone had dropped out (no pun intended).

REJECTION SENSITIVE DYSPHORIA AND IMPOSTER SYNDROME

As this girl sat there expressing her disappointment that she would have to cancel the trip, I heard myself saying, on complete impulse, "I'll do it!" The girl was delighted and declared me a "life saver!" and a warm feeling of being valuable and liked swept over me.

The next morning, I woke up, went downstairs and saw an envelope on my doormat with the information about "The Jump" stuffed into it. "Oh shit!" I thought. I really, really didn't want to do it. But I was so worried about how I would be perceived if I broke my promise.

A few weeks later, I was up in Cambridge for the weekend of "The Jump". The first day comprised of intense training, which started with us jumping off boxes on to crash mats. "I can do this", I reasoned with myself, but by the end of the afternoon I was absolutely terrified. We had been told how to pull the reserve cord if our parachutes failed, and been warned of broken limbs if we landed incorrectly.

The next morning, we woke up to drizzle and wind. The people I was with were concerned that "The Jump" would be cancelled due to the weather. I prayed the weather would get worse! It didn't.

Several hours later, we were up in a plane, 3000 feet up, parachutes strapped to our backs. I still couldn't believe I was doing this. I was utterly petrified. I didn't want to do it, but was more scared of people being disappointed in me for not doing it than I was of jumping.

We were doing static line jumps, so were jumping out alone, with it drilled into us that we had to count to five, and if our parachutes didn't open, we had to deploy our reserves. I was so scared when I jumped that I got to "ten" before I opened my eyes to check if my chute had opened!

I then experienced a brief feeling of complete euphoria; I was amazed as a bird actually flew past my face as I floated down to the ground. Then I remembered I had to land!

I did land, unscathed, feeling an overwhelming sense of relief that I was still alive and a sense of pride that I had done it, and that I had not let myself or anyone else down.

Remember those lovely "friends" at school who used me as their lunchtime lackey? Well, although no crime was committed, I do feel, looking back, that these girls really took advantage of me. I believe that children and adults with ADHD are particularly susceptible to being taken advantage of due to our people-pleasing ways and impulsivity. (Worryingly, this could lead to even further abuse, such as "mate crime", which neurodivergent individuals are more likely to be victims of.)

I think people with ADHD can become very vulnerable to abuse and are incredibly susceptible to being used and exploited by others. We are generally extremely kind-hearted and generous, and our RSD means we don't want others to be disappointed in us, so saying "yes" to others and impulsively not thinking through the consequences of our actions can potentially lead us down unhappy and treacherous paths.

Here are some things my mouth has instantly replied "Yes, of course!" to when actually my brain was saying, sometimes screaming, "No, I don't want to...":

"Lend us £20, Lor?"
"You can babysit for us on Friday night, can't you?"
"Can you give us a lift so we can go and pick up some weed?"
"It's okay if I don't use a condom, isn't it?"

Since my diagnosis, I have learned, with the support of my neurodivergent friends, that it is okay to say "no".

I have learned that people will respect you more for being honest, and although it feels a bit scary to put yourself first, I promise you will probably find you stop overcommitting and start prioritizing your needs over other people's, which will only be beneficial to you in the long run.

Learning how much ADHD has affected my need to please others has led me to realize the following:

- I've learned it's more important to be respected than liked.
- I've learned that I can stand up for myself, and it actually feels good when I do.
- I do still worry a lot about what people think of me. I have accepted that I will always be highly sensitive to

criticism and rejection – that's just the way my brain works.
- I've learned that putting myself first doesn't make me selfish; it makes me happier.
- I have learned that I don't need to jump out of planes to be a good friend.

Understanding that our ADHD means we experience RSD and can be people pleasers can help us self-advocate and protect ourselves from being taken advantage of.

> "In my younger years, RSD used to trap me in a mindset of 'people think I'm bad, I'll be bad'. As I've matured, self-awareness helps me recognize these self-sabotaging tendencies, although resisting impulsive reactions remains a challenge. Yet my children act as my protective factors, preventing me from 'acting out', particularly in my work roles, because the consequences would affect them as much as me."
>
> RSD

LOUISE

Imposter syndrome

If RSD were a person, I think they would be a bit like Miss Trunchbull from *Matilda*, or that horrible boss at work, putting you down and bullying you all the time and making

REJECTION SENSITIVE DYSPHORIA AND IMPOSTER SYNDROME

you feel like crap! Now, RSD has a really annoying cousin, imposter syndrome (who I think sounds like another bad superhero character from the film *The Incredibles*).

Throughout my adulthood, and particularly in working environments, I have experienced terrible imposter syndrome, which is closely interlinked with my RSD.

This has resulted in awful anxiety throughout my professional life that I am a fraud and a fake, about to be exposed, that I'm not good enough, and that I shouldn't be doing the job I do.

For me, imposter syndrome is not as severe and brutal as RSD, but it is a constant, nagging doubt in the back of my mind, like a mosquito buzzing about in a room at night.

Imposter syndrome makes you doubt yourself and your strengths; it makes you feel as though you are not quite good enough, that you aren't really deserving of your accomplishments and that you "cheated" or "tricked" your way to success.

If you have ADHD, then you probably experience imposter syndrome at times, and if you do, then you are in good company. Michelle Obama, Lady Gaga, Emma Watson and Jodie Foster are just some of the incredibly successful women who have spoken out about experiencing imposter syndrome.

As I have already explained, the term "imposter syndrome" was coined by clinical psychologists in the 1970s. They used it as a way to describe how certain people find it hard to recognize their achievements, despite evidence that they are indeed successful.

> In their 1978 paper entitled "The impostor phenomenon in high achieving women: Dynamics and therapeutic intervention", Pauline Clance and Suzanne Imes wrote about a group of 150 women who were considered successful and experts in their fields: "despite their earned degrees, scholastic honors, high achievement on standardized tests, praise and professional recognition from colleagues and respected authorities, these women do not experience an internal sense of success. They consider themselves to be 'impostors'. Women who experience the impostor phenomenon maintain a strong belief that they are not intelligent; in fact they are convinced that they have fooled anyone who thinks otherwise" (p.1).

Imposter syndrome makes you feel like a fraud, with constant anxiety that you will be "found out", and it means you cannot accept that your success is real and deserved as a result of your hard work.

You may be in the "imposter syndrome club" if you experience the following:

- Finding it hard to believe or recognize that your success was as a result of your effort, talents or hard work
- Focusing on the times that you didn't do well rather than the times you did and were successful
- Attributing your success to other reasons or other people, rather that recognizing your own role in success
- Spending a lot of time comparing yourself to others and thinking that you are not as "good" as them (remember that "Comparison is the thief of joy"!)
- Finding it hard to enjoy or celebrate your success.

"**People seem to see me very differently than I see myself. Would love to be able to get over this feeling!! As I age, I'm getting better at believing in myself.** There's just so much noise around us all the time, telling us how to think, encouraging us to constantly compare ourselves to others in the culture of competition in which we live; this doesn't help."

KATIE

It is no surprise that people with ADHD experience imposter syndrome. We are likely to already be hiding our authenticity and masking our difficulties from others, particularly in social or work settings. Not being authentic in itself makes you feel fraudulent and like an imposter.

> "Imposter syndrome is misleading...it isn't about feeling like you don't belong; it's about being made to feel like you don't belong because either you aren't accepted as you are, or you aren't surrounded by people who are like you. When I was a child, I had that feeling of being 'too much, too loud, too intense...' because no one around me was like that. As I got older, I found myself gravitating toward people who were like me, or appreciated that quality in me, and I never felt that way again."

IRIS

Like most of us with ADHD, I have experienced imposter syndrome in so many aspects of my life.

When I won a gold medal at a gymnastic competition as a child, I told myself I only won as some of the other competitors had been ill that day.

When I won a local business award, I told myself I had only won because one of the judges had an autistic grandchild and was biased towards me.

When I was a head teacher, I was enrolled on a course entitled "National Professional Qualification for Headship" (NPQH). Just getting on to the course involved two days of interviews. I remember sitting there looking at the other delegates thinking to myself that they all seemed so much "better" than me. I was surprised to be accepted on to the course, which was incredibly hard work, and spent the whole time I was doing it thinking "I should not really be here". When I called to find out if I had passed my NPQH and was told I had, I shouted down the phone, "Oh my **god**! Thank **god**!", which made the lady on the other end of the phone laugh and question why I was so surprised!

Not long after I became a head teacher, we had a successful Ofsted inspection at my school. I told myself we only did well as I was still riding on the wave of the previous head teacher. I spent my whole time in that job thinking that I was going to get "found out". I was looking over my shoulder the whole time for the person who was going call me out. It made me feel so anxious every single day.

> "Imposter syndrome is something that I struggle with. I feel this way when I am around people that are more educated than I am, when I don't feel like I can keep up with or understand what people are talking about, and I feel this way when it comes to advocating for my child. I worry about whether or not I am knowledgeable enough to speak out, or if I am being irrational or overly emotional about a possible (or a very real) injustice. It's hard to feel confident about what I want to say when I feel anxious and imposter-y, and so sometimes I may avoid situations where I feel 'unqualified' to be part of a conversation."
>
> STEPHANIE

When my first book was published, I remember thinking that it was only really a success because my lovely friend Eliza had illustrated it, and that I had just ridden on her coat tails.

Sitting here now, typing this, I am thinking, "What gives me the right to write this book, when there are thousands of other women who could probably do a better job?" (I hope if you have got this far, you aren't thinking the same!)

Basically, I was unable to accept that any of my accomplishments were because I was actually good at what I was doing. I just doubted myself and my abilities all the time.

I even experienced imposter syndrome when I got my ADHD diagnosis. I sat on the sidelines of the online groups I had joined, too anxious to comment or post in case I said something that made me look stupid or fraudulent. I am not alone in feeling this way about my diagnosis.

> "I have also had challenges with imposter syndrome related to my diagnosis. This is due to the stigma of what autism or ADHD should look like. Again, even though diagnosed, I can sometimes get this feeling of 'I'm making it up' and that I somehow managed to trick professionals into thinking I was neurodivergent."
>
> **LOUISE**

REJECTION SENSITIVE DYSPHORIA AND IMPOSTER SYNDROME

Once I learned about imposter syndrome, it was almost a relief to learn that there is a name for the way I was thinking, and that it was my brain playing tricks and lying to me.

When that annoying, niggling voice tries to trick me into thinking I am not good enough, I remind myself that it is just the way my brain is wired. I remind myself that I am successful, and that I am good enough.

I find the evidence that cancels out the doubts and of all the times I have proved that annoying voice wrong. It's still a work in progress, but I am slowly getting there. I have also realized that the more I embrace my ADHD, the more authentic I become, and the more authentic I am, the more successful I am too, and this is something we can all do as women with ADHD.

"I don't have imposter syndrome with the drawings and paintings that I produce, because I know I'm very good at it. My dad was a professional artist and illustrator, so I've grown up in that world; art comes very naturally to me and I'm confident in my abilities. With other things in life that I have to try harder at, there's definitely imposter syndrome getting in the way. I am aware of it, however, and that's extremely helpful in working to overcome it."

LUCY

WHAT ELSE COULD HELP?

With RSD

- ✓ Remind yourself of the times when your brain tricked you – for example, that time when you thought someone hated you because they hadn't texted you back and then you found out they had lost their phone! This is **evidence** that your brain is lying to you sometimes.
- ✓ Try "thought changing" when your brain takes you down those destructive paths. Remind yourself of happy, positive times. Your brain can only have one thought at a time, so push the negative thoughts out and replace them with positive ones.
- ✓ Talking therapy can really help, but make sure the therapist really understands ADHD.
- ✓ Use scaling to reframe the severity of the RSD. If something felt like a 9/10 on the criticism scale, then your RSD has probably really ramped it up when it was more like a "5". It can help to think about this when you are not dwelling on the incident or event that has made you feel so worried, or you can discuss it with a friend when you are feeling calmer and ask them how they would rate it. This is not intended to invalidate your feelings, but to remind you that at times your brain is tricking you into thinking things are worse than they really are.
- ✓ Don't be scared to tell people you are feeling RSD. You can always send a text message saying

something like "The RSD is really RSDing today – just wanted to make sure you had seen my message and you don't actually hate me 😊!!"
- ✓ Remember that no one is perfect all the time; there is not an adult human being out there who has not made mistakes, pissed people off or been annoying, sometimes.
- ✓ Journaling can help you process your feelings, and it can also help you keep evidence of all the times your brain tricked you and you got it wrong.
- ✓ Embrace the fact that you are a really sensitive person. Yes, this means you will experience RSD sometimes, but I bet it makes you a really amazing person in other ways too.

With imposter syndrome

- ✓ An ADHD coach or therapist who really understands ADHD can point out things you may be doing that are a result of imposter syndrome.
- ✓ Again, as long as they really get your ADHD, a CBT (cognitive behavioural therapy) therapist can help you identify your negative thoughts and focus on your positive ones. They can also help you see that many of the negative thoughts you have are untrue and are lying to you. CBT does not work for everyone, and if you are also autistic, you will definitely need a CBT therapist who is fully understanding of your neurotype.
- ✓ I know I keep banging on about this, but comparison

really is the thief of joy. Stop comparing yourself and your achievements, or perceived lack of them, to others. There will always be others who have achieved more than you.
- ✓ Write down or record your achievements. You don't have to show these to anyone; they are just for you to look at to remind yourself that you are a capable and successful human being!
- ✓ Repeat positive affirmations to yourself about your achievements. No, you are not going mad if you talk to yourself – sometimes you actually need to give yourself a good talking to!!
- ✓ Learn to accept positive feedback. People are not just humouring you or patronizing you – you deserve it.

Chapter Five

Work and Career

Professionally, our difficulties linked to our ADHD, such as RSD, imposter syndrome, poor executive functioning and difficulties with attention and processing, mean we have to work harder than our neurotypical colleagues to achieve the same results. This is something that others overlook, as we also do ourselves.

In addition to these challenges, I have had many disasters at work that I can attribute to my ADHD. Before my diagnosis, these mishaps continued to reinforce the

WORK AND CAREER

self-imposed narrative of myself as being clumsy, stupid, disorganized, and therefore unprofessional and not really quite good enough.

Some of my recent highlights include:

- The time I hurriedly parked on a member of staff's bag in a school car park, which included their trousers, so they had to ask me to move my car so that they could get changed for work.
- The time I delivered training to a packed room with toilet roll hanging out the back of my trousers like a tail (and didn't notice until halfway through the training when a kind person pointed it out). Mortified is an understatement!
- The time I delivered training at a college with horse poo smeared up my arm as I had not allowed enough time to muck out my horse before going to work. (And did not realize until I got home, although I did notice a strange smell while I was delivering the training.)
- The time I did a face-to-face consult with a family with a smear of chocolate on the end of my nose as I had been running late and rushed out of the house before checking my appearance. It looked like poo.
- The time I got called "Karen" at the start of a consult and was too embarrassed to correct them, so they just carried on calling me Karen all the way through, and then in subsequent email correspondence. Moving forward, I toyed with the idea of signing off

my emails "Kind regards, Karen", to save both our blushes.
- Most recently, I got the heel of my shoe caught in a grate in a school playground five minutes before I was due to deliver training, which resulted in the grate coming out of the ground completely and the lovely SENCO (special educational needs coordinator) at the school and me both wrestling with it and finally managing to rescue my shoe. I don't know what I was more embarrassed about – my unintentional snowshoe creation or the state of my toenails that had not been "done" for months!!

Clearly, I am not alone in experiencing embarrassing workplace mishaps.

"I worked in a secondary school and I needed to speak to the head teacher and knocked on his door. He asked me to come in and I did, but once inside the office I could not remember what I was there for. Now bear in mind I'd had a knee op two years prior and had had limited mobility for a while. So instead of just walking out like any other person would, I said, 'Oh look, John, my knee's better', while doing lunges in front of him. I left the office and was mortified. Why would anyone do that? Now I know why!!!"

SU

WORK AND CAREER

Like many women with ADHD, it seems that we flit from job to job, finding it hard to settle down into one career for long.

> "My jobs have included: market stall worker, pie maker, pot wash, airport worker, barista, bar maid, sandwich maker, retail sales assistant, personal shopper, cash office worker, electrical production line worker, department store sales assistant, premiership football club marketing assistant, student, photographer, Alaskan sled dog handler, kennel hand, veterinary care assistant, waitress, pet store employee, artist and writer. My CV alone tells its own exhausting tale – no single workplace disaster, just a pathway littered with a desperate search for happiness and fulfilment. I leapt from one job to another as my emotional dysregulation, RSD and frustration with other colleagues always landed me in hot water."
>
> JODY

I dabbled with the idea of lots of jobs as I was growing up. I wanted to be a paediatrician for some time, but realized I wasn't cut out for the academic side of that.

I then decided to be a nurse, but realized I wouldn't be good with blood and gore. At one point, I decided to be a vet but, again, wouldn't cut the mustard in the brains department, and ditto the issue with blood and guts. I also realized I would become a snivelling wreck if I ever had to put an animal to sleep.

I went through a particularly religious phase in my early teens and decided I wanted to be a nun, but that went out the window when I discovered boys!

> "I've done so many jobs! I've struggled with burnout in every single one. I'm terrible in an office. I'd get headaches from the lighting and often distracted colleagues because I'm unable to focus, stay on task or get started. The only job I lasted in was one where if I didn't, I'd lose my house and be homeless. I was able to work from home in that job and spent most of my time on visits and hiding from my team because I couldn't cope with being in an office. It exhausted me and I had no idea why."

SARAH A

I think now that the career I have forged is perfect for me because it is linked to the things I am passionate about, and this is essential for us as women with ADHD. I have always been interested in psychology and behaviour, and also wanted to work with children too.

I did my degree in psychology, which I loved, apart from statistics! (God, how I hated the statistics!!!) I have always been interested in crime and serial killers, so dabbled with the idea of going into criminal psychology, but this would have meant years of further studying (which, of course, I was too impatient to do), so I gave up on that idea.

I left university with a 2:2 (also known as a Desmond (Tutu)), which my friends and I convinced ourselves was the best grade, telling each other that employers wouldn't want a graduate with a "First" as it looked like you were really boring and didn't have a good work/social life balance. A "Desmond" showed you were bright enough to get a degree, but also knew how to party – essential skills for any workplace, of course.

The summer I returned home from university, I was restless, and spent hours writing over 40 letters to prospective employers for various research jobs and work within the field of psychology. I received about four replies, all rejection letters.

I eventually got a job as a care assistant in a residential care home for adults with disabilities. During my interview, I spoke about how interested I was in psychology and behaviour, and how I felt my skills would be well utilized in the role.

I arrived incredibly eager on my first day, to be given a scrappy bit of paper with a list of my jobs. Most of the jobs involved supporting adults with personal care, including their toileting needs. Within a few hours of being there, I was helping a lovely man get ready for the day ahead, when his very full catheter became detached and sprayed all over me. I was absolutely mortified and was allowed to go home to get changed out of my urine-soaked clothes. I cried as I drove home and had to literally force myself to get in the car to go back. I couldn't believe I had worked for three years at uni to get a Desmond, only to be wiping people's bums and changing beds.

I only really enjoyed one element of the job, and that was getting to know the residents. Many of them had been in the home for years and had very little contact with their families. I used to spend time chatting with them, until I was hauled into the office one day by the senior manager who told me that I was "overfriendly" and needed to spend less time chatting and more time working. I was fuming. I also hated the way that some of the other care workers treated the residents; I felt that they treated them with disrespect, and even ridicule at times.

Desperate to leave, I had an interview with a local recruitment company and was told about a job going with a local estate agent. I was sold by the fact that this job came with a company car! I went for the interview and was offered the job.

Being an estate agent meant I worked incredibly long hours, including Saturdays and some Sundays. The hourly rate was appalling, and the commission was very slow in coming, not good for an impatient ADHDer with a penchant for impulse buying! I also found the job very pressurized and began to feel anxiety every time I drove past a "For Sale" sign in my little company car (that I managed to knock the wing mirror off on my first day – you know spatial awareness isn't my biggest strength) as I would be reminded of the houses I was yet to sell. I realized being an estate agent was not for me, so back to the recruitment company I went.

The second time I sat in that recruitment office, I was offered a sales and marketing role at a courier company. Desperate to leave the estate agent, I impulsively took the job, but again ended up hating it, so found myself back in the recruitment office for a third time and took on a role that meant I jumped out of one job I was desperate to escape from into another which, once again, I hated. I think when you have ADHD, the feeling of being trapped is overwhelming and suffocating.

> "I couldn't function in a 9–5 job, and I felt trapped... truthfully, I was a terrible employee. Bored, unchallenged, unsupported. I was desperate to leave and used to call in sick all the time."
>
> IRIS

As women with ADHD, we need our work to be stimulating and exciting, and we get bored easily, so the initial excitement and dopamine hit of a new job wears off quickly;

before we have our feet settled under our desks, we begin to get restless and want to move on again.

> "I have had many experiences of being really excited about a new job, and then becoming disillusioned with it later. I think maybe sometimes I got bored with the work, and other times I realized I didn't like the people I worked with or the work I was doing. I had a couple of jobs I wanted to quit, but didn't have the courage to say so and ended up ghosting my employers."

STEPHANIE

At the age of 26, I realized that I was jumping from job to job and was miserable. The dread of Monday mornings started to creep into my weekends, around Saturday evening, and I felt completely rudderless and unfulfilled. I left my awful sales and marketing job and trained to become a teacher, and the moment I walked into that classroom, I knew I had found the thing I wanted to do. I absolutely loved my job, and finally felt that I had found my vocation. For someone with ADHD, doing something you love or are passionate about is essential.

I loved my job as a tutor. After a few years, I became a manager in a specialist college, then an assistant head teacher and then head teacher at a specialist school for autistic children. As I explained in Chapter Four, though, I never really felt like I was "good enough" to be head teacher.

And although I loved teaching and being with the students, I did really struggle with being a manager of staff.

I am very conflict-avoidant and a people pleaser, and working in a school meant dealing with a lot of low-level conflict a lot of the time (student vs. student, student vs. staff, staff vs. staff and staff vs. parent!). I felt like I was constantly firefighting and never able to please all the people all the time.

Walking into the staff room, I assumed most of the staff disliked me. I now realize I was actually very unwell for most of the time I worked in my school. I was anxious most days and lost a huge amount of weight. I also realize that I was heavily masking, literally donning a uniform of a suit and heels each day and going into the role that people assumed I should be. It was exhausting.

> "Recently, I was asked to provide a professional development session to paediatricians and allied health at a public hospital. I am well qualified and have the lived experience to deliver a presentation, but my imposter syndrome prevents me from believing that they meant it when they extended the invitation, and prevents me from reaching out to organize it. Somehow, I don't quite believe that I can do it."

SARAH B

> "I struggle massively with rejection sensitive dysphoria, and this creeps in a lot in my job. If a client doesn't book on, or a new person comes to class and I never see them again, I spend days worrying and going over everything I did. Did I say something wrong? Did my 'weirdness' put them off me?"

SARAH A

I left teaching and set up my own business and became self-employed in 2013. I can honestly say that working for myself is the best decision I have ever made. I love the autonomy that being self-employed gives me, and I am also incredibly lucky to do a job that is linked to my strong interests in behaviour, education and neurodiversity.

I think self-employment is a way of working that really works for many of us with ADHD:

I now actually credit my ADHD with the success of my businesses, and know that the drive and energy I have is largely due to my neurodivergent brain. Once we understand our brains, we can use our different way of thinking to our advantage, and this is where success kicks in.

Being self-employed does still have its challenges, and many of these are part of my ADHD.

"Life changed when I became self-employed. The hardest thing has been choosing what to focus my energy on. I'm now a Pilates instructor, specializing in rehabilitation, so I really feel like I'm helping people and making a difference. I can put my mask on for the time I'm with clients, and then take it off for all the background admin and planning I do. I work from home or in venues I choose, and I'm able to constantly go on courses to improve my knowledge. It's not the best-paid job – in fact, I've taken a massive pay cut – but I'm happy."

SARAH A

"ADHD has helped me to see gaps in the market; I see things others don't. My hyperfocus helped me to upskill at incredible speeds!"

IRIS

My organization skills, or lack of them, have been a constant challenge for me in most of the jobs I have had. I have a habit of double-booking appointments, which makes me feel really panicky, or committing to too many things, and then feeling utterly overwhelmed and scared of letting people down.

My ADHD means that I am usually rushing about, and not

really paying attention to my surroundings. It's amazing I am still in one piece, really!

One of the questions that really stood out to me when I finally had my ADHD assessment was "How often do you feel overly active and compelled to do things, like you are driven by a motor?" This really resonated with me as I do feel like sometimes I am not in control of the speed I go at, and this is definitely the case when I am completing tasks. It means I rush, make careless mistakes and sometimes omit essential stages of tasks.

My executive functioning is really awful, particularly when I am stressed, and the more stressed I am, the worse my executive functioning becomes. Our difficulties with executive functioning mean that we are more likely to make mistakes at work, which again compounds our feeling of being "imposters".

> "When I worked in investment banking, I sent one of my senior sales traders to a client meeting in a completely separate venue to that which I sent his client to. That senior sales trader then got me fired. He wasn't someone to cross. Constant silly little mistakes that, despite double-checking work meticulously, I still make. I don't understand why it happens, but now attribute it to my ADHD and my need to be doing lots of different things at once."

KATIE

Because of my ADHD, I am so easily overwhelmed by too much information, and a full inbox of emails will make me panic as I find it hard to know where to begin. I also hate receiving long emails that are not broken down, and find it impossible to read a "wall of text". If I get an email like this, I tend to look at it, think "nope" and then mark it as unread.

Reading anything too long and boring (including something I have written myself) is a challenge, and I tend to skim-read most things, which means I do miss important details at times. I also have a tendency to jump from task to task. I will start doing something that then triggers a memory that I need to do something else.

Here is an example of how easily I can go off-task:

1. Read an email from a school confirming details of upcoming training that also asks if I need anything printed off.
2. Think to myself, "Oh, I could print that off myself to save them a job, but we probably need more printer ink." Don't bother to check the printer ink as it is too far to walk to the end of the garden where the printer is located, in my husband's office cabin.
3. Go on to Amazon (other printer ink websites are available) and notice that I have cat litter in my shopping basket that I have not checked out.
4. Go to the cupboard to see if we need any other pet supplies while I am purchasing cat litter.

5. Go to feed the cat as he has heard me open "The Cat Cupboard" and now expects food.
6. Notice the cat litter tray needs emptying and proceed to do so, but spill cat litter on the floor. Go to get the hoover to clear up the cat litter, notice the battery of the hoover is flat, so go to charge that up in the kitchen and notice the washing machine has finished, so start to hang washing...

Two days later, I receive another email from the school asking me, again, to confirm training details. Then RSD kicks in and I decide the school must think I am terrible and unprofessional and probably won't book me again for training.

As an ADHDer, when a thought, idea or memory of something I need to do pops into my head, I have to act on it immediately. If I don't, it will disappear. But it doesn't disappear completely; it leaves a residue behind, like a kind of "vapour", so then I get anxious because I know I have forgotten something. I get distracted by the "vapour" because it lingers around, slightly out of reach, sometimes giving me a little glimpse or clue of what I need to do before evaporating again. This means I have to act on things immediately, or I have to write them down. Or, when the "vapour" clears and the memory or thought reappears, I have to jump on this too.

"I sometimes experience the frustration of having profound insights in sessions and then forgetting them midway. Over time, I've learned to let it flow and trust that the thought will return. Organization remains a struggle, but using large whiteboards for reminders has proven to be a significant game-changer."

LOUISE

I will often reach for my phone just as I am drifting off to sleep to check an email I realize I have forgotten to reply to or a task I need to do. I have to check or make a note on my phone, as it will keep me awake if I try to hold it in my head until morning. In meetings, I have learned to write copious notes or bullet points because I can keep track of the thoughts as they float in and out of my brain, but in conversations in social situations, this is much harder to do. I know I interrupt a lot, because if I don't, then the thing that I want to say will disappear, but I try **really** hard not to do this as I know it can come across as rude.

I can easily lose the thread of conversations if I am trying too hard not to interrupt and keep the thing I want to say in my head before it leaves again. When you have ADHD, your thoughts and ideas can be really hard to hold on to. So when we interrupt, call out or appear to act impulsively, we are not doing it on purpose, but it can appear that we are being rude or disrespectful; we are just desperately trying to grasp the thought or idea before it vaporizes or disappears.

> "I worry constantly that I will forget something. At home, I'm very scatty, but I can't be like that at work so I am meticulous with checking to make sure I have fulfilled expectations."
>
> RACHEL B

I try to counteract my tendency to lose thing by putting them in a "really safe place". I then forget where the "really safe place" is and end up losing them. This is extremely frustrating, but it is quite exciting when I find things again, often months later!

As I have already said, one of the biggest myths about ADHD is that it is an "attention deficit" disorder. A lot of the time, I don't have a deficit of attention; I have too much attention, but I just can't apply evenly to tasks I need to work on.

If I am interested in something, I can hyperfocus like you would not believe! My friends at uni used to joke that if I was reading something I found interesting, I would become so engrossed they could drop a bomb next to me, or wave wine, chocolate or a cigarette under my nose, and I wouldn't notice.

When I am hyperfocusing, I become time blind too, literally losing all sense of time. This can sometimes have dangerous consequences, and it is quite miraculous that I have not burnt my house down as I will often start cooking, and then think to myself that I will just check an email and get completely engrossed until I smell burning!

People who have ADHD are much more likely to experience time blindness, which can present as:

- Finding it hard to work out how longs tasks will take to complete
- Easily losing track of time
- Finding it hard to stick to schedules
- Finding it hard to be punctual for an event.

> Interestingly, time blindness is not just thought to be a result of poor executive or cognitive skills, but is also a sensory-related difficulty. Time blindness is linked to the scalar expectancy theory, or SET, as explained by Chara Malapani and Stephen Fairhurst in an article they wrote in 2002. SET is like an internal clock that allows people to understand the concept of a minute of time passing linked to the beating of their heart. As we are so easily distracted when we have ADHD, perhaps our brains are unable to accurately notice or track our internal clock, and we also don't notice the other things going on around us that indicate the passing of time.

When I am hyperfocusing or concentrating, I get really irritated when I am interrupted. It is very hard for me to get back in my flow state, and as an ADHDer, I have a high degree of monotropism.

> Dinah Murray, Mike Lesser and Wenn Lawson developed the theory of monotropism (name drop – Dinah Murray was, coincidentally, my tutor when I did my postgrad in autism in the 1990s). Their work was first published in 2005, and is now being continued by Dinah Murray's son, Fergus, as well as others.

The first time I read about monotropism, it was like another lightbulb moment. It didn't just explain so much about the autistic clients I have worked with for so long, but also so much about me! I did a "monotropism quiz" online and scored very highly!

"Mono" means single and "tropic" means tunnel, so the theory of monotropism means that some people find it really hard to focus their attention on anything outside a single tunnel of interest. Although this theory was initially developed as a theory of autism, it is also highly relevant to people with ADHD. It can explain why we hyperfocus, because we get caught up in our "flow", but also why it is so hard and requires so much effort to do things we basically have little or no interest in, and why we will delay and procrastinate in undertaking some tasks.

Being taken out of my monotropic flow state is very

frustrating. When I am in my flow state, I would describe it as riding the most comfortable bike downhill on a lovely smooth road – it just feels so easy and effortless. Being yanked out of my flow state is similar to my bike going off the road and having to peddle up hill on a bumpy and overgrown path – it's just really, really hard work, and not very enjoyable!

> "Learning about the value of flow states made a huge difference to how I existed in the world... When you are young, you are often told that the things that interest you are weird. Or you are told to stop going on about them all the time, so you learn to hide your excitable energy because it is inconvenient to others. As an adult, I have managed to create a successful career for myself by focusing on the things that I find interesting, and earning a living from them."

IRIS

I need my work to be stimulating and exciting. This is why I love doing assessments and school observations, as I have to really use my brain. I also enjoy training and public speaking as I can "perform". But, like many ADHDers, I do experience demand avoidance over things that I perceive as "boring".

Report writing is something I tend to put off and procrastinate over because I find it really demanding.

I have done the interesting, stimulating part of the work (the assessments, etc.), but then the report part is tedious and requires really good concentration, so I get mentally paralysed and feel I just can't start. This is until my people pleasing kicks in, and I panic that people will be disappointed or annoyed with me if I don't pull my finger out!

I have a complete inability to read Excel spreadsheets, let alone use them effectively. I know some people **love** a spreadsheet, but as soon as I am asked to look at one, or input data into them, my brain just thinks "nope". Anything to do with finance and numbers, I instantly swich off at and develop mental paralysis again, so I send them over to my brilliant bookkeeper who sorts all these elements of my work and keeps me on the straight and narrow tax-wise!

> "My job also requires me to be constantly moving and talking. Something I'm very good at. I now employ an accountant, so I don't lose my mind trying to do my books. It's not that I can't do it – I can – I just find it so tedious! I also use an online booking system. It loses me money but saves my sanity from trying to manage all my clients!"

SARAH A

For some people with ADHD, "body doubling" can be really

helpful when completing tasks that they find challenging. This is not some type of paired WWF wrestling term, but is a method of working in the presence of someone else. The presence of the other person can help you stay on task and reduce distractions. Sometimes just having someone else with you can help you stay regulated and calm when completing frustrating tasks too.

I have now been self-employed for almost 11 years, and I love it. I cannot imagine working for anyone or having a "boss" again. I work with people I like, doing something I love. I can set my own schedule and take time off when I need it without asking anyone for permission. I love the autonomy I now have, and every week is different, which I also love, although it means I never really have a routine – which is both a blessing and a curse!

I have a PA, which someone referred to once as a "luxury". My PA is **not** a luxury; she is an absolute necessity. I also have an accountant who deals with anything related to tax, HMRC or invoices. There have been months when I have paid my PA and accountant more than I have paid myself – crap business modelling, I know, but there would not be a business if I had to do it all myself!

I work extremely hard, and sometimes need to re-establish my work-life balance. I have been described as a workaholic on many occasions. Yes, work is also stressful at times, but then, if it wasn't stressful, I would be bored, wouldn't I?!

I think I will be like my dad, who is still working and self-employed at the age of 81!

> "My role now, in the charity sector, works much better for me. I plan my own calendar for the majority of each week. I have so much autonomy. There are deadlines, but things don't have to be done in certain ways. I have always thought I either work at 200% or 10%, and the freedom in my job now allows for that. I also have a wonderful manager I can tell when I am having an unproductive day, and he supports me or tells me to take some time off. He is happy with the work I do; I do it well and get it done, just maybe in a less typical way."

CATHERINE

I really believe that the key to success as a woman with ADHD is embracing your ADHD, recognizing your strengths and accepting the things you find hard, being able to self-advocate, and finding something you love.

> "My ADHD without doubt has also helped me in my work and past career as I was so driven by my hyperfocus. I never knew the whys of it, but I loved the buzz of focusing on something so intensely. Now I know my strengths so much more, I'm able to choose between things that make me avoidant and

instead try to only do things that drive that hyperfocus."

MICHELE

WHAT ELSE COULD HELP?

✓ If you are employed, ask for a meeting with your supervisor or manager regarding reasonable adjustments that you are entitled to and need.
✓ Put an "Out of Office" message on your emails that you have always on, which states that you may not respond to emails immediately, to give yourself more time.
✓ Tell people what you need to make your job more accessible, such as asking for emails to be broken down into smaller chunks. Don't be scared to explain how you need information sent or presented.
✓ Set timers on your phone for breaks and to break up your hyperfocus and help with time blindness.
✓ Play background music that is set for certain chunks of time (30 minutes, 60 minutes, etc.) to help remind you to take breaks and also to help with time blindness.
✓ Schedule breaks in your day to allow for catch-up time if your hyperfocus means you overrun.
✓ Don't see success as "finishing" but starting a task – this will make you feel you have achieved more and prevent you from giving up.

- ✓ Break tasks down into smaller, more achievable chunks that you can tick off as you complete them.
- ✓ Use visual aids such as colour-coding or Post-it® notes that you can keep around you and then throw away when you have completed a task.
- ✓ There are some great apps or electronic planners that you can use to help you track tasks and deadlines.
- ✓ Use your phone for reminders and set alarms for important meetings or events.
- ✓ Make a "To Do" list on your phone or in your diary.
- ✓ Plan ahead so that you have everything ready the night before, including your outfit!
- ✓ Ensure you carry things in your bag so you don't get caught out (like sanitary products or a spare phone charger).
- ✓ Consider using reading or dictation software.

Useful links

For advice on reasonable adjustments at work

Acas offers employees and employers free, impartial advice on workplace rights, rules and best practice: www.acas.org.uk

Government advice on reasonable adjustments for workers with disabilities or health conditions: www.gov.uk/reasonable-adjustments-for-disabled-workers

For advice on access to work

Government advice on Access to Work:
www.gov.uk/access-to-work

If you are experiencing sexual harassment at work

Women Against Abuse (a US site) strives to provide a continuum of care, from telephone crisis counselling to long-term supportive housing, in a manner that promotes victim safety, autonomy and dignity:
www.womenagainstabuse.org

Chapter Six

How to Manage the Ups and Downs of ADHD and Mental Health

Living with ADHD, particularly undiagnosed ADHD, can result in masking, RSD, imposter syndrome and anxiety. These all become intertwined and can result in us experiencing poor mental health, something so many of us experience as women with ADHD.

> "Being ADHD, particularly undiagnosed ADHD, has significantly affected my mental health over the years. I have spent my entire life feeling stressed, panicked and overwhelmed. I feel like I have been running on adrenaline for 45 years, which has made it very hard to find any kind of 'inner peace', sense of ease or happiness."

RACHAEL

As I mentioned in Chapter One, I didn't realize how anxious I was as a child, but now, looking back, I realize that I was an **extremely** anxious child. I had "butterflies" in my tummy almost permanently; I didn't realize that this was not normal, that there was another way to "feel".

> "I have always been anxious. Always. I could never work out why I worried about things others didn't seem to, and on some level it has always controlled my life and the things I choose and choose not to do."

CATHERINE

I now realize how much anxiety my ADHD causes in me as an adult. People don't think I am anxious because I do a lot of public speaking, but when I am up on stage, or the spotlight is on me when I am presenting online, I am playing a role. I never understood why I was so tired after delivering training or presentations, until I realized that I was usually doing this behind a mask, pretending to be a confident woman I rarely felt I was!

> "Having ADHD means I have to work harder at many things that other people seem to find easy. In my work, I overthink and overplan. But I get good results generally, so people seem to have high expectations of me. So when I come to do something again, it takes a lot of effort and time to get it right. People, including myself, often tell me that I need to put more effort in, but actually I think I have to put an awful lot of effort into life already. It is exhausting."

MIRIAM

Masking is also known as camouflaging and is used to describe a person acting in a way that is more "socially acceptable" to blend or fit in. When we have ADHD, this means we have to control our impulsivity, behave in a way that is not authentic and copy those around us to feel more accepted. We may also feel that we cannot fidget or move around, and may also suppress our true feelings or emotions because when we do, they are invalidated by others.

We mask because we don't feel safe or comfortable to be our true authentic selves. Masking is bloody exhausting, but then not masking is really frightening as we may feel that people won't like us or accept us, or our behaviour may not be deemed "acceptable", particularly when we are with new people or in a new working environment.

> "It's really hard to differentiate between the two intertwined entities of ADHD and our mental wellbeing; as a 51-year-old woman, this is a literal minefield that I am constantly revisiting with a fine-tooth comb, all the while expecting explosions. Every one of us late diagnosed is constantly unpacking the devastation in the rear-view mirror, a task that rewards with equal measure of relief and grief. I now realize with palpable sadness how early in life my anxiety actually began, how I carried it, and used shame to keep it hidden, so no one would ever discover the truth."
>
> JODY

Masking can really impact our mental health and can contribute to burnout too. It is well documented that adults with ADHD are more likely to experience mental health difficulties.

> Depression is estimated to be 2.7 times more prevalent among adults with ADHD than among the general adult population. Studies published in *ADDitude Magazine* also show that about 30% of people with ADHD will experience a depressive episode or have a mood disorder in their lifetimes (Sherman 2019).

When I was a child, my undiagnosed ADHD led to me developing some behaviours and characteristics that I now recognize as obsessive-compulsive disorder (OCD). My tendency for forgetfulness and absent-mindedness has led to an overwhelming anxiety that this will lead to me not doing things, which will lead to disaster.

> **"I derived more comfort from organizing my toys than playing with them, and by puberty I had absolutely developed a form of OCD and had begun, without even realizing it, to pull out my own hair in times of stress. I was subconsciously exerting control over a chaotic, undiagnosed, neurodiverse household, managing the unending upswell of panic that accompanied the reality that my mother, my supposed safety net, couldn't boil an egg without nearly burning the house down."**
>
> JODY

One of my first pets was a hamster I named Watford (after

my favourite teacher's favourite football team). One night, I forgot to shut his cage properly, and he escaped and ate my bedroom curtains. My mum wasn't too happy about this, but Watford was, as he made a very cosy bed out of the chewed-up curtains. After this, I was so worried about forgetting to shut the cage again that I developed an elaborate bedtime routine that included checking the cage about ten times, and I could not go to sleep until this had been done.

I also developed a fear of not shutting the front door of my childhood home properly. I would worry that I had left it open and would catastrophize that I would come home from school or college to a house that had been burgled, and our family dogs would have all escaped and been run over. This meant I would start walking to school or to the station to catch my train to college, and then have to run back home again to check the front door was actually shut (it always was).

I now have a fear of leaving my hair straighteners on and burning my house down. My poor mum has had to drive round to my house on numerous occasions to check that they are off, and guess what? They always are!!

When my anxiety is high, my need to check things increases. I was once eating dinner in a restaurant with a friend who worked in a similar field to me. We were talking about safeguarding and the need to keep confidential files locked away. At the time, my anxiety was really high, and her comment planted a seed of doubt in my mind that I may not have locked my filing cabinet in my office at the school where I was working at the time. I could not get the thought out of my head, and could not relax and enjoy my meal, so eventually I excused myself and drove back halfway round the M25 motorway at 10.30 at night, let myself into my school, which was absolutely terrifying when it was dark and empty, and checked my cupboard. Guess what? It was locked!!!!

Before my ADHD diagnosis, I would deny my anxiety existed, and I now realize how unhealthy this is.

About ten years ago, I had a really significant and traumatic event at work. I had to leave my job as a result and became very unwell. I kept pushing on and, a bit like when I had postnatal depression, saw my anxiety and subsequent depression as something that I just had to get over. I told people I was okay when I wasn't, and kept on pushing myself through. I was not sleeping at all and was so low that I even thought that it may just be easier to not be alive anymore.

Months went on with me feeling like this, until one day I was sitting at some traffic lights and the car impatiently hooting behind me jerked me out of the trance I was in; I also then realized I had tears streaming down my face. I finally went to my GP who diagnosed me with severe anxiety and depression, and prescribed me fluoxetine. I remember thinking that it would not work, because the underlying cause of my anxiety and depression would still be there, but after three weeks I woke up one morning and realized that I was going to be okay.

I only stayed on fluoxetine for about a year, but I honestly don't know how I would have got through that period of my life without it. It's not for everyone, but medication can really help some of us with ADHD who struggle so much with our mental health.

> "I am on medication long term for anxiety. I have tried to come off it two or three times now, but things crumble when I am not on it. For me, the medication helps keep me as even as I can be, which is still pretty much a rollercoaster, but a more manageable one!"

CATHERINE

Although times are changing, there is still a stigma attached to mental health. Most of us don't think twice about booking a GP's appointment when we are physically unwell or in pain, but I know a lot of people who soldier on for too long when they are mentally unwell.

I have now accepted that I am an anxious person and probably always will be. This year, I started seeing a therapist for the first time in my life, which has been incredibly helpful. She is neuro-affirming and really seems to understand my ADHD. She has picked up on my tendency to catastrophize and also, interestingly, suggested that I may be an empath, which has explained a lot too.

Because of my ADHD, I am highly sensitive and hyperempathetic, which means that I can be really sensitive to other people's emotions. I hate being around people who are angry as it makes me very anxious. But other people's sadness really impacts me too. If people cry around me, I have to try really, really hard not to cry myself.

As a neurodivergent human, I just feel my emotions in a really, really big way, and always have. When people tell me things like "Come on, it's not that bad" or "Stop overreacting" or "Calm down", I feel completely invalidated and it does not help me in the slightest. (Seriously, though, when has anyone who has been told to "calm down" felt calmer?!)

As I explained in Chapter One, when I was a child, I would cry very easily if I was upset (I still do). This was sometimes misinterpreted as "attention seeking", sometimes even manipulative, as I was seen to be trying to garner sympathy to distract from my misdemeanours.

When I have lost people or pets, the grief I experience is literally unbearable. I feel grief so, so strongly that it causes me physical pain and leaves me unable to sleep, eat or even breathe properly for weeks, and it has made me question if I am "normal" to have these reactions.

Similarly, if I am looking forward to something, the excitement can become so much that I will lie awake at night for days beforehand. This often leads to crashing disappointment and either sadness or anger as things don't always measure up to my expectations.

It is essential for us to remember that, as neurodivergent adults, there is no such thing as an overreaction for us; what we feel is just that, what we feel, and it can be really helpful for us to explain to this to our friends, family and colleagues so that they don't invalidate our responses. We also need to make sure we don't invalidate ourselves too. If people misjudge our reactions and we are invalidated, we will not get the correct support, which is very damaging to our self-esteem and mental health

Using some assertiveness techniques can be really helpful in making sure our responses are taken seriously and not invalidated. I have found this one really helpful to use, both verbally and in written responses, such as emails or text messages:

> **When you:** Don't respond to my text messages...
> **I feel:** Anxious and worried that I have offended you.
> **I need you to:** Just send me a quick note to let me know everything is okay.

Or:

> **Fact:** When you shout, it makes me feel really stressed.

Sympathy: I know you are angry right now.
Solution: Let me know when you are feeling calmer and ready to talk.

When I was diagnosed with ADHD, the psychiatrist prescribed me a stimulant medication.

I took it for a few days and **hated** how it made me feel. Although my productivity went up significantly, I felt like I wanted to crawl out of my own skin, I felt more anxious and nearly chewed my own tongue off I was gurning so much! I also could not sleep, which is something I struggle with anyway.

The sensation of taking these drugs, which are basically amphetamines, was not dissimilar to that which I experienced in my raving days, so after a few days I decided to give them up. A few of my fellow ADHD friends told me I should stick with it, but, ironically, I was too impatient to give my ADHD meds a chance to work.

A lot of my friends with ADHD have described their medication as "lifesaving" and "transformative", and I know some friends who say that they could not function without it. I think it is just important to do what is right for you, and speak to your GP or psychiatrist if you feel that your meds are not having the desired effect.

Research carried out by ADHD UK in 2011 states that 54% of adults in the UK with an ADHD diagnosis are in receipt of medication. I think this shows that medication is not for everyone, but for those who do take it, it can be really helpful (ADHD UK 2024).

I was not alone in finding medication difficult to tolerate. A study by Thomas Spencer, Joseph Biederman and Timothy Wilens in 2004 stated that "While there is no doubt that the stimulants are effective in the treatment of ADHD, it is estimated that at 30% of affectedindividuals do not adequately respond or cannot tolerate stimulant treatment".

"I have been medicated with ADHD meds for approximately 18 months and the difference has been profound. For the first time in 37 years, I am not being driven mad by my own thoughts, by the constant anxiety and overwhelm. For the first time in years, I sleep more than 3-5 hours a night, I have been able to maintain a healthy weight, I have better relationships with my children and husband, and engage with life in a better, heathier, more positive way than I ever have before."

KYRA

It is also important to know that it can take time to find the right medication for you and that there are different types of medication; the stimulant/amphetamine meds don't work for everyone as they can raise anxiety. There are non-stimulant types that may be more suitable for you if you experience a lot of anxiety, and it is worth exploring this with your GP or psychiatrist.

> "I started taking ADHD meds about 18 months ago and while I don't think they have a huge effect or are life-changing for me, I definitely feel that they help me to feel more regulated and less overwhelmed."
>
> COURTNEY

I have found that CBD oil has really helped me with anxiety, but it can be hard to find information about the correct dosage to take. I have also taken beta-blockers if I know that I have something that makes me anxious coming up. Beta-blockers don't stop the psychological symptoms of anxiety, but they do slow your heart rate, which can make you feel much better.

I try to manage my mental health using more natural methods now, too. I definitely see an increase in my anxiety when I have been drinking too much alcohol and not getting enough sleep. I have to force myself off my phone at night as this definitely impacts my sleep, and have found that listening to audiobooks helps me sleep better. Exercise, even just walking, also really helps me, so I do try to go for a walk most days if I can.

Another strategy I have found helpful to combat my anxiety is by finding the "glimmers" in my life.

> The concept of "glimmers" was developed by Deb Dana and is linked to the Polyvagal Theory, which was coined by Stephen Porges in 1995. This theory explains that we are always scanning our environment for danger, whether we are conscious of it or not. Deb Dana introduced the concept of "glimmers" in her 2018 book, *The Polyvagal Theory in Therapy: Engaging the Rhythm of Regulation*.

We all have our individual anxiety triggers, and glimmers are the antidotes to our triggers. Whereas triggers activate our nervous system, glimmers can help calm them down. Just understanding the way our brain works and perceives threats can be a huge help in supporting our mental health as women with ADHD.

Our nervous system is active when we perceive a threat, whether it be real or not. So, for example, I will be activated by someone behaving in an aggressive way (a real threat) and equally activated if I think I am going to be late (a perceived threat). My cognitive and physiological anxiety response is the same.

By the same token, we can calm our nervous system if we think about or experience something that makes us feel happy or safe – these are our glimmers.

My glimmers include:

- The back of my cat's fluffy head
- Hearing my children laughing uncontrollably
- Seeing bulbs shooting after a long winter
- Windy walks along the beach
- Sitting outside in the sunshine with a cup of tea first thing in the morning
- Listening to music (this can be classical or an amazing house music track)
- Cuddling up on the sofa with my dog.

If I can spend time engaging in these things, or even just thinking about them, I will feel calmer. I think a lot of us with ADHD find peace in nature and being outdoors.

> "Spending time outdoors, in nature and with animals, has always been a special interest for me. Growing up, we always had many types of animals, from cats and dogs to birds, lizards and chameleons, to name a few. I guess they have been important to me because of the feeling it has always given. Being in the presence of animals just makes my heart feel happy and connected. As an adult, I simply could not be without dogs – the bond and unconditional love is like medicine to my soul."

MADDIE

Another strategy I have learned that has been really helpful is going to my "happy place". I actually have two "happy places". One is a private island in the Maldives, and one is a private garden in a hotel in Mallorca.

Now, I don't actually have to get on a plane and travel to these places to experience them. I can just close my eyes and really imagine I am there.. I do this by imagining:

- What I can see
- What I can feel or touch
- What I can smell
- What I can hear
- What I can taste.

I can trick my brain into thinking that I am back in these places, and then I can't think about the things that are making me feel stressed or anxious because my brain cannot hold two thoughts at the same time (the same way a radio cannot play two channels at the same time).

My "happy places" help me tune out the unwanted thoughts and voices in my head, and can help me sleep sometimes when I have insomnia. It takes a bit of work, but it has been really helpful to me, particularly during times of high anxiety and stress.

One of the things I struggle with most having ADHD is that it is almost impossible for me to stop, rest and "do nothing". When you have ADHD, it is really, really hard to switch off

– even when our bodies are resting, our brains are still on the go.

> "I never rest. I am either on the go, coming up with grand plans (which normally involve spending money to start something I never finish), feeling like I need to do something but not knowing what to do or being in burnout where I can do nothing at all. The anxiety is crippling. I'm always anxious – I have many anxiety attacks a day. I wear the most excellent mask and there is only one person on this earth who knows the true me – my husband."
>
> NIKKI

I mistake the need to rest with "being lazy", and I keep thinking about everything I have to do, and I feel guilty thinking about not doing "something" all the time.

When I was younger, my mum would regularly tell me I was "burning the candle at both ends" and I needed to slow down and take it easier. Of course, I did not listen to her and would often end up really unwell and unable to get out of bed for days. I didn't know then that what I was experiencing was "burnout".

Even now, I still take on too much, on a treadmill of relentless work, social and family commitments, and then end up crashing and need a day in bed doing nothing to recover, but lying there feeling so guilty that I am not busy doing something.

Burnout is a term I am sure many of you are familiar with, because ADHD and burnout are really common. Even if you didn't know it had a name, you have almost definitely experienced it!

> "In my adult life, I have almost always been in some level of burnout. But even though I now have self-awareness, it's really hard to drop the 'fawn mask'. I've been doing it for so long it's become part of me. It's second- nature. It feels almost impossible to drop the thing that keeps me safe."

RACHAEL

We are really susceptible to burnout due to our people pleasing, masking, procrastination and avoidance, issues with timekeeping and time blindness, and lack of structure and routine in our lives.

Symptoms of burnout are different for everyone, but can include:

- Feeling completely exhausted
- Needing to sleep more, and wanting to stay in bed
- Feeling easily overwhelmed
- Becoming less tolerant of others

- Isolating ourselves from others
- Finding it hard to communicate with others
- Feeling that you have no motivation to do anything, including things you usually enjoy
- Feeling more emotional and reacting more than usual
- Increased demand avoidance
- Loss of appetite or comfort eating
- Having difficulties with executive functioning, concentration and processing
- Difficulty making decisions (not always easy when you have ADHD anyway!)
- Feeling less inclined to look ourselves properly – that is, personal hygiene.

I have friends who have been diagnosed with depression who were actually experiencing burnout. They are two completely separate conditions – although you can have burnout without depression, it can lead to depression. To me, burnout is an environmental and lifestyle imbalance, and as neurodivergent people, our environment is often not adapted to our needs.

Although it can be hard, we do need to listen to our bodies and take burnout very seriously because it can become debilitating, and long-term stress is really bad for our bodies and our mental health.

ADHD means we can easily get into a cycle of behaviours that lead to burnout.

What has helped me the most with managing my burnout is recognizing that "resting" does not necessarily mean doing nothing or sleeping. For me, resting can be going for a walk, meeting a friend for coffee, or it can be working on my doll's house (have I mentioned I have a doll's house yet?).

As a woman with ADHD, it is important that you find **your** way of resting, which may look completely different to other people's.

> "Quiet time is essential for me for better wellbeing. I need a period of silence and no demands every day. I am usually the last one up at night and have time then, but if, for whatever reason, that doesn't happen, I know the next day will be a struggle."
>
> CATHERINE

Another really important way I have managed to navigate burnout is by learning to say "no". I have already covered this in Chapters Two and Four, but this has become an essential word for me to be able to say, so that I don't take on too much.

I have also implemented tighter boundaries around my work. At one point during the first Covid-19 lockdown, and prior to my diagnosis, I was working ten- or 12-hour days, every day. I was accepting any work I was offered as I was so terrified my business would go under. My days and evenings were completely full. I remember one of my stepdaughters seeing my calendar and being really shocked at how full it was. Some days I would not even have time for a lunch break. Needless to say, that did not end well, and I was a snapping, irritable, erratic and tearful mess most of the time.

Healthy routines and structure can help us avoid burnout, and I now have a much more defined and more structured working week. I have a lunch break that is scheduled into my calendar every day, which I really try not to miss, and I now only work one or two evenings a week and try to have one admin day per week. I have learned that it is okay to say "no" or "not yet", and that the work is still there, even if people have to wait a little longer for me to complete it.

Planning ahead and being organized can also help us avoid burnout. This is something I have had to program myself to do, but it has really helped. If I see I have a busy week, then I try really hard to make sure that the following week is a little quieter.

I have also learned that it is okay to admit I am struggling and to ask for help. Again, this is something I find hard to do. I must admit I have been a bit of a martyr in the past and seen asking for help as a sign of weakness. I was wrong on this! Being honest about the fact that I am struggling is almost always met with understanding. Dropping balls and making mistakes, less so.

Finally, a really important way to avoid burnout is by identifying the things that deplete my reserves and the things that replenish them. This leads me nicely on to "spoon theory".

The first time I heard someone say they were "low on spoons", I thought that they must have kids who threw the teaspoons out with their yoghurt pots (very annoying). I quickly realized, however, that they were talking about a completely different type of spoon.

> The "spoon theory" was created by Christine Miserandino in 2003 as a way of describing how much mental energy she had. Christine is a lupus sufferer and found "spoon theory" a really helpful way of telling people that she was running low on energy. The term has now been adopted by the neurodivergent community, and is a really easy way to express how you feel when you are getting tired or feeling overwhelmed (Wikipedia 2024).[1]

In spoon theory, one "spoon" is like a unit of energy. So, for example, you will wake up each morning with a certain number of "spoons". Demands, expectations, tasks and jobs will use up your "spoons" until you run out, and when you are "out of spoons", you won't feel like you have any energy left.

---

1   See https://butyoudontlooksick.com/category/the-spoon-theory

Again, everyone is different, but it can be really helpful to identify what uses and replenishes our spoons to help us plan ahead and reduce the risk of burnout.

Examples of things that use up my "spoons" are:

- Attending meetings with lots of people
- Public speaking and training
- Using public transport
- Going to the supermarket
- Reading long, boring emails
- Social situations where there are lots of people I don't know
- Not taking enough breaks in my work day.

Some of the things that replenish my spoons are:

- Walking my dog
- Being in nature
- Spending time on my special interests
- Clothes shopping (more on this later)
- Watching rubbish reality TV (yes, I love *Love Island* and *Big Brother*, and I am not ashamed to admit it!!)
- Going out for dinner with my husband
- Being with one or two close friends rather than a large group.

Identifying these things is so useful in helping me plan and regulate myself. If I know I am doing a lot of the stuff in the first list, I will try to intersperse it with things from the second.

I have also started to say to my neurokin that I am "low on spoons" and I know that they get it (and are not about to suggest I go to a store to get some new ones!).

Finally, I have come to accept that anxiety will always be a part of my life. I am learning that I will probably always feel anxious because that is how my brain works. This has really helped me feel more regulated, rather than setting off a spiral of further anxiety. Just telling myself that I feel anxious because of my brain, rather than because there is something "wrong", has been really useful and has reduced that feeling of impending doom!

WHAT ELSE COULD HELP?

- ✓ Try to get regular exercise – even just walking for 20 minutes a day can give you a dopamine hit.
- ✓ Try to avoid alcohol or limit alcohol consumption to weekends only or special occasions.
- ✓ Eat regular, healthy meals and cut down on sugar as this can impact mood and sleep patterns.
- ✓ Get plenty of sleep. Try to turn off screens at least one hour before bedtime to reduce the impact of blue light.
- ✓ Try listening to audiobooks or meditation apps to help you sleep.

- ✓ Have a short power nap in the day, or even just at weekends, to ensure you are well rested.
- ✓ Identify what "rest" means to you. This can be spending time on your special interests or hobbies.
- ✓ Identify what uses your "spoons" and what depletes them.
- ✓ Identify your "glimmers" and try to find your "happy place".
- ✓ Journaling may really help you identify your problems, fears and concerns, and it can help to process these feelings by getting them "out" of your head and on to paper.
- ✓ Writing your concerns down can help you to separate your "worries" and your "problems". Remember, worries are not real; problems are.
- ✓ Make time for yourself. Don't overcommit and don't be scared to say "no" to people. Use the assertiveness techniques given earlier in this chapter.
- ✓ Speak to your GP if you feel you are struggling or are feeling overwhelmed.
- ✓ A neuro-affirming therapist could help you offload and offer solutions-based support.
- ✓ Approaches such as Emotional Freedom Techniques[2] (EFT) can help with anxiety. Cognitive behaviour therapy[3] (CBT) can be helpful as long as it is adapted for your neurodivergent needs.

---

2 See, for example, https://en.wikipedia.org/wiki/Emotional_Freedom_Techniques
3 See, for example, www.nhs.uk/mental-health/talking-therapies-medicine-treatments/talking-therapies-and-counselling/cognitive-behavioural-therapy-cbt/overview

- ✓ Eye movement desensitization and reprocessing[4] (EMDR) and brain spotting[5] can be very helpful to help process trauma.

Useful links

The Association of Mental Health Providers (Women's Mental Health) is the national voice of mental health charities, providing services in England and Wales: https://amhp.org.uk

Mind highlights how supportive and reliable information can change someone's life: www.mind.org.uk

To find a counsellor or therapist

Counselling Directory: www.counselling-directory.org.uk

---

[4] See, for example, www.bacp.co.uk/about-therapy/types-of-therapy/eye-movement-desensitisation-and-reprocessing-emdr
[5] See, for example, www.verywellmind.com/brainspotting-therapy-definition-techniques-and-efficacy-5213947

Chapter Seven

Friendships and Relationships

Like many ADHDers/women with ADHD, my older teenage years were when I found my people. The first time I felt that I really "belonged" was when I discovered the rave scene at the age of 16. I found myself in a community where everyone seemed equal and accepting. We all had one goal – to stay up for as long as we could, dance all night and chat utter bollocks to as many people as we could until the early hours. Perfect for someone with ADHD! I actually met some friends through this scene who are still my best friends to date.

I have never really had problems making friends. I am probably described as a very friendly person, and I am very lucky to have many amazing friends in my life – some of them I have known for over 40 years. But there have been many casualties along the road of friendships.

Before my ADHD diagnosis, which led to the recognition of negative patterns I was repeating, I had a tendency to meet people and then throw myself very impulsively and very quickly into friendships without taking the time to really get to know that person. In the process, I have been hurt many times, something that seems to happen to many of us with ADHD.

> "Growing up, I never felt adequate within friendships. I would feel overly sensitive, paranoid, overthink situations where I worried I'd said something in the wrong way, or behaved in a way that was frowned upon. I would overanalyse situations again and again in my head until I couldn't even remember that situation accurately, and then the cycle would continue as my changing memory over what happened would make me even more anxious. The pattern would repeat itself over and over."

MICHELE

As I said in Chapter One, I had a really awful time at my secondary school and didn't really fit in at my private girls' school, so the first time I really felt that I fitted in was when I went to university. The friends I met there are still some of my best friends today.

I have always found it hard to say "no" to people for fear of upsetting them or them leaving me. This has meant that I have often put other people's needs before my own, which has led to me being and feeling used and taken advantage of.

> "When I was younger and before my diagnosis, my people pleasing definitely meant I did not always have good boundaries and I have been taken advantage of. I often felt weird and annoying and a bit 'too much' at times too."
>
> SARAH A

I am also very conflict-avoidant, so if people upset me, I would avoid discussing things for fear of it causing an argument, only to brew in simmering hurt and resentment until I finally blew up and, in the process, blew the friendship up too.

Before my diagnosis and before I understood RSD, I had a fear of people not liking me. For some reason, people liking me was overwhelmingly important to me. Sometimes my new friendships would take on an almost obsessive form. I would feel extremely jealous of my friends' other friends. I would also adapt aspects of myself to be more like people in the hope that they would like me more. I would copy people's clothes, musical tastes, etc. I now recognize that, like so many of us with ADHD, I was masking to fit in.

> "I have a tendency to speak without a filter, especially if I've had a drink or two. Some of my inappropriate comments have caused friction in relationships and friendships."

SARAH B

> "As someone who has masked heavily all through my life, I have found it hard to let people see the 'real' me. Consequently, I've been seen by many as a quiet, shy, introverted person – which is absolutely not the case! I knew in my heart that I was a different person to how I was being perceived but I didn't know why I couldn't let people see the real me. I was just too anxious."

AMY

Now I understand my ADHD and myself so much better, I have definitely become more protective of myself in my friendships. I do recognize my worth, and that if other people don't see that, then they don't deserve to be my friend.

I am now far more guarded in my friendships, and can categorize people as "radiators" and "drains". I only need people in my life who radiate and give back, and I certainly don't need the "drains" who just take and give nothing back. This has led me to have fewer friends, but much, much better ones.

> "I'm a lot older now and I have a solid circle of friends where the relationships are reciprocal. But it's taken me such a long time to get here."

IRIS

Most of my friends now are neurodivergent. I don't "pick" people based on their neurotype; I have just realized that I feel most comfortable around others who share one that is similar to mine. Having friends I can be completely authentic around is so important, and something that seems to be vital to us as ADHD women.

> "Once I found out I was ADHD, I realized that other neurodivergent people made me feel safe. And of course I then realized that a lot of my friends were also neurodivergent! Now that I understand myself and why I've had trouble in the past, I can move towards that feeling of safety and make sure that I can be my authentic self with the people that matter most."
>
> AMY

When I was younger, a lot of my friends were boys. Having three brothers who always had lots of friends over to our house meant that I was very used to being in their company. I also found boys less complicated than girls.

I met my first proper boyfriend when I was about 15. He was the same age as me, but at the age of 15 he looked considerably older as he was Italian and blessed with a face of stubble, which came with the added bonus that he could get served without ID in most pubs. He was known to some of the girls in my school as being quite a catch, and some of them had already "got off" with him at parties.

I met him at our local under-18s nightclub, Cinderella's, and could not believe it when he expressed an interest in me. We started "going out" and had a really lovely summer, but I spent the whole time we were together not quite believing I was worthy of his attention. (Bloody Kevin clearly did some damage!) I remember once we were sitting in a park having a picnic when he told me that I would be "beautiful" when I was older. Although he meant it as a compliment, I remember feeling wounded that he meant I was not beautiful now. Our relationship was initially quite innocent and involved lots of snogging, which meant I had a permanently sore face due to the Italian stubble.

The more his feelings seemed to grow towards me, the more and more insecure I felt. I then sabotaged the relationship by pulling away completely and ignoring his phone calls. He told a friend of mine years later that I was his first love and that I had broken his heart.

I met my next serious boyfriend at the Reading Festival. This relationship involved a lot of raving and recovering together. Very quickly, it turned more into a friendship, and ended when I was at university.

I had a few dalliances with fellow students at university, but seemed to be stuck in a pattern of meeting guys who were not after anything serious, jumping in too fast, and having high expectations of the relationship, meaning I got my heart smashed a few times.

I then started seeing someone from home. I had been fairly obsessed with him since I was younger, mainly due to his prowess on a skateboard. He was the most unreliable person I had ever met, due to his serious cannabis habit and the fact that he was still in love with his ex. He would promise me he would come and see me at the weekend, and then fail to turn up. My friends could see that he was treating me appallingly, but I always forgave him, desperate for the tiny bit of attention he paid me. I now see that this treatment of me has a name, "breadcrumbing".[1]

After I left uni, I started seeing another guy from home. He initially pursued me relentlessly, despite me not being interested in him. Then, once I succumbed to his charms, he became completely disinterested, but also really possessive. This was probably my most damaging relationship. I lost all my self-respect to this man.

The most common attachment style for people with ADHD is insecure attachment. This is hardly surprising when you put together our feelings of being different, RSD and imposter syndrome.

I now understand that I have a very anxious attachment style in my relationships with the opposite sex and even in some of my friendships.

Features of insecure attachment include:

- Fear of rejection
- Feelings of jealousy
- A need for constant reassurance
- Low self-esteem

---

1   See, for example, www.verywellmind.com/what-is-breadcrumbing-5220677

- Trust issues
- Abandonment issues
- Problems with trust
- Highly sensitive to criticism.

Looking back at the relationships I had in my late teens and early twenties, they were all very unhealthy. I always went for the "bad boys". I was utterly turned off by nice men who would have treated me well. I allowed myself to be treated very badly, always giving so much of myself with very little in return. I can see now that the way I allowed myself to be treated made me insecure, needy, obsessive and possessive, and this created a vicious circle that was really hard to break. If I could, I would go back and give myself a big shake and tell myself I deserved so, so much better, something I suspect a lot of us wish we could do.

> "In relationships, I often put myself in toxic ones, where I people-pleased above how I truly wanted to behave or where I truly wanted to be. Having the attention, even in ways that may not have been positive for my reputation, gave my insecurities what they needed to feel – the temporary 'love' and affection I craved."

MICHELE

> "In terms of relationships, I have definitely used them to give me validation rather than because they were healthy for me. I also spent some time in my early twenties engaging in some risky behaviour without thinking of the consequences – chasing the dopamine and hyperfocusing on particular people or experiences."
>
> GEMMA

A little while ago, I spent the weekend with two other neurodivergent women I had recently met. As we chatted about our past, something shocking revealed itself. We had all been sexually assaulted at some point in our lives, and some of us more than once.

> Sadly, this is not uncommon for women with ADHD. Young *et al.* (2020) stated that "Females with ADHD overall have an earlier onset of sexual activity, more sexual partners, and an increased risk of contracting sexually transmitted infections or having an unplanned pregnancy. They are at risk of sexual exploitation, perceived exhibitionism or being considered promiscuous" (p.21).

It is probably no surprise to you that the divorce rate of couples where one party has ADHD is high. Rushing impulsively into relationships, dopamine and excitement hunting, RSD, masking, being forgetful or "unreliable", and all the other ingredients that can make up ADHD, are not always going to create the recipe for a perfect marriage, particularly when ADHD is not diagnosed.

> "I think I was very promiscuous when I was younger and seemed to use sex as a way of connecting and I suppose masking. It was easier to have sex than conversations. I have been in risky situations where I have been taken advantage of sexually, and one very frightening experience that I have never really addressed."

LOUISE P

> "One trivial ADHD quirk that has a tendency to annoy partners is that I leave cupboard doors open without realizing. Most likely I have retrieved what's needed from the cupboard, and my thoughts have moved on before I remember to close them. I do tend to leave unfinished tasks around the house that I will get back to in time. It's like there are multiple projects on the go, but none of them are finished."

SARAH B

Estimates vary, but some studies suggest that the divorce

rate among couples where one party has ADHD is as much as twice that of the general population.[2]

> "Luckily, I am now with a partner who I've known as a friend for many years. It's very healthy and we are very good for each other. I have also found my own tribe of what I would call gloriously wonky friends, and a business partner who is very similar to me. It's taken me a while (till my forties!) to realize that I didn't have to spend time with people who made me feel bad about myself, or people that I thought I should be friends with but were actually not meant for me."

GEMMA

So, I am part of that statistic, and my first marriage did end in divorce, but I am now happily married to Steve #2.

Steve and I met online not long after my first marriage ended. I wasn't really looking for anything serious and was looking forward to enjoying being single for a while and finding myself again. But the first time I met Steve, we just clicked. I made a vow to myself that I would be completely "myself" around him, and he seemed to like the authentic me. Marriage isn't always easy, there are always ups and downs, but Steve is loyal and predictable and is very good at

---

2   See www.additudemag.com/adhd-marriage-statistics-personal-stories

housework and loves hoovering, which is a massive bonus as I hate it. He also loves me for being "me", and I think this is the first relationship where this has ever been the case.

WHAT ELSE COULD HELP?

- ✓ Learn to put yourself first and listen to your gut. Pay attention to how friendships make you feel. If you feel a rush of anxiety when you see certain numbers come up on your phone, then you need to listen to this. If a friendship or relationship feels toxic or unhealthy, it probably is!
- ✓ Remind yourself that you are not responsible for other people's actions or behaviours.
- ✓ Use the assertiveness techniques from Chapter Six to help you communicate how you are feeling if friendships or relationships are making you feel anxious or unhappy.
- ✓ Explain what you need from friendships and relationships by using the assertiveness techniques from Chapter Six.
- ✓ Don't beat yourself up if a friendship or relationship ends. Remember, it takes two people to make a relationship work, so don't blame yourself if things don't work out.
- ✓ Some friendships will fizzle out. This is normal and it doesn't make you a bad person just because a friendship ends.
- ✓ Take time to grieve and process when a friendship or

relationship ends rather than rushing into something new to fill a void.
- ✓ Identify the "radiators" and "drains" in your life, and remind yourself that friends should be about quality, not quantity. Don't feel bad about walking away when you know that a friendship has run its course.
- ✓ Learn to put healthy boundaries in place, and don't get drawn into other people's toxicity or dramas.
- ✓ If you need to take some time to yourself, or don't want to accept an invitation, just explain your reasons for this. A good friend will understand and respect them.

Useful links

For victims of domestic violence

Government guidance on domestic abuse: www.gov.uk/guidance/domestic-abuse-how-to-get-help

Women's Aid is a national charity working to end domestic abuse against women and children: www.womensaid.org.uk

Women Against Abuse provides quality, compassionate, and non-judgemental services in a manner that fosters self-respect and independence in those experiencing intimate partner violence: www.womenagainstabuse.org

Woman's Trust is a specialist mental health charity,

providing free counselling and therapy for women in London who have experienced domestic abuse: https://womanstrust.org.uk

For victims of sexual abuse

Government sexual abuse support: https://sexualabusesupport.campaign.gov.uk

Rape Crisis, a feminist charity working to end child sexual abuse, rape, sexual assault, sexual harassment and all other forms of sexual violence: https://rapecrisis.org.uk

The Survivors Trust is a national membership organization supporting specialist rape and sexual abuse services in the voluntary sector: www.thesurvivorstrust.org

Chapter Eight

Impulsivity and Impatience

ADHD and impulsivity – it's a double-edged sword! Although some of my best decisions have been very impulsive ones, this has not always been the case. I think my impulsivity is a thread that weaves through every part of my life as a woman with ADHD.

"Impulsivity and impatience are my main ADHD symptoms. When my daughter was diagnosed and I looked up signs of ADHD in women and girls, the bit that described interrupting other people when they were talking was the deal breaker for me. All my life I have had to interrupt, blurt out, talk over, say my thought, no matter how inappropriate or rude. I have always known it is wrong, rude, obnoxious and widely disliked. No one hates the trait in me more than I hate it in myself, and yet…"

DEBORAH

"I am incredibly impulsive, and as a child, I was so unsafe…because I didn't understand it and I hated feeling caged in. As an adult, it's allowed me to continuously thrive in my career and experience so much joy in life. It's not all sunshine and rainbows… I've definitely had to take it on the chin occasionally, when an impulsive act hasn't paid off…but the benefits of embracing that impulsivity far outweigh the cons."

IRIS

ADHD is also so contradictory at times. I can be very impulsive and yet also get so stuck in procrastination and monotropic hyperfocus at times. It's like my brain and body are just out of whack sometimes. You know when you type really fast on a keyboard, and you type faster than the computer can keep up with and there is a lag with the words appearing on the screen? That is like my brain sometimes, and I am sure many of you can relate!

> "I've always been a very impulsive person, see things and need them immediately. Want to start a project or do something, well, it all needs to be done yesterday. I'm very impatient, and if it is a task I am unable to manage myself, and no one will help me, you can be sure that I will find a way to start it. When I was teenager, I definitely acted on impulse more than people around me. I didn't know then that it was part of ADHD. I've always had a 'live in the moment' attitude, think about the consequences later. Impulsivity has definitely always given the dopamine rush that I was chasing. I wish I'd had a better understanding of this, as at the time I'd think 'What is wrong with me?' Why can't I resist the temptation to jump in and do something?"

MADDIE

IMPULSIVITY AND IMPATIENCE

My impulsivity has led to the following:

- Deciding on my way to the hairdressers for a trim and highlights that I would actually suit a peroxide-blonde pixie cut. (I didn't, and I cried for weeks!)
- A kitchen cupboard full of various weight-loss shakes that I've impulsively bought after seeing Facebook ads. (Honestly, I **will** start my healthy eating/weight-loss diet one day!)
- An embarrassing amount of clothing I didn't need and rarely wear.
- Regretting at least one of my tattoos.
- Numerous beauty products in my bathroom that I probably only used once.
- Jumping into agreements without thinking them through or reading the small print.
- Writing this book!

Both inattentive and hyperactive-impulsive subtypes of ADHD are prone to impulse control problems.

> A study by Teresa Bailey and Arthur Joyce in 2015 found that a part of the brain called the thalamus may be responsible for impulsivity in ADHD, explaining that the thalamus sends messages to the prefrontal cortex, which is responsible for executive function. When the messaging doesn't work properly, there may be a delay in executive functions, such as impulse control.

> "Before I was diagnosed with ADHD, I always saw myself in a perpetual state of fast-forward and rewind. Always making decisions before fully contemplating their consequences, then having to rewind and unravel those decisions that were made in haste."
>
> **HEATHER**

Like many women with ADHD, I have always been terrible with money.

> "I normally spend money on impulse. These purchases have included family holidays abroad (without consulting family), a newer car, even though I had one which ran perfectly fine. I am the only driver at home so I would swap them after a few days as I was too attached to let the other car go! My best one was when I returned from my part-time job one night with a gorgeous German Shepherd puppy. My parents had no idea until the following morning as I had sneaked her upstairs into my room. I was allowed to keep her; we named her Tara."
>
> **LESLEY**

My best/worst impulsive buy was a very expensive French Bulldog puppy. Luna was a living, breathing example of my impulsivity.

IMPULSIVITY AND IMPATIENCE

One day in February 2019, I impulsively decided we needed another dog. We already had one French Bulldog, Rocket (AKA "the most perfect dog in the world"). We had lost our 17-year-old Border Terrier, Bertie, the previous November, but only having one practically perfect dog was just too easy!

As we went out for dinner that night, I announced to my husband that I thought we should get another puppy, stating that Rocket was lonely and would appreciate the company. "Rocket is fine, but we could think about getting a dog in the summer holidays when you have a long break," Steve replied.

I said I would message Darren (AKA Rocket's breeder, and not the object of my crush from school) **just** to see if he had any puppies due for the start of the summer holidays. About three minutes later, a message and video came back of a four-month-old puppy who was meant to be going to South America as a show dog, but apparently the deal had fallen through.

"Ooooohhhhhhhhhh!!! Look, Steve!!!!" I cried, thrusting my phone in his face as he tried to drive. "This puppy is available now!!!" Steve was absolutely adamant that it was too soon and that we should wait until the summer. Two weeks later, I drove to Luton "just to have a look", and guess what? I came back with Luna! And Rocket really was delighted!!!!

Unfortunately, Luna had a lot of health issues. I don't think she was ever destined for South America, and I think the breeder knew she wasn't quite right and couldn't sell her to a more discerning and less impulsive customer. I rushed into this purchase without pausing to check everything, and sadly we lost Luna when she was just five years old due to her health issues, which I am still broken-hearted about.

> "My most impulsive action was probably buying a horse with money that I had been saving for a deposit on a house. It was a ridiculous and expensive thing to do. He was an ex-racehorse, I had ridden him once and he refused to trot over poles that were on the ground, without a huge fuss. However, I didn't regret it. He was the best horse. A real gentleman. We had many happy years together. I was very lucky that this didn't backfire, and would not recommend people buying animals impulsively. But when I saw he was for sale, I just knew he was the horse for me. However, ask me to choose what we should have for dinner tonight, and I won't be able to decide!"
>
> MIRIAM

Some of my **best** and most creative ideas are also the result of my impulsive brain. Ideas for webinars, courses, posts, support services, etc. spring into my head when I least expect them. Some of the best decisions I've made in my life have also been intuitive and impulsive.

This book is actually a result of my impulsivity. Later on in this book (if you get that far), you are going to read "The tale of the missing black top!" As I recounted this tale to my friend Eliza, who illustrated this book, on our way out one evening, she told me, "Oh my God, you have to write about this!" and the idea for this book was born. I came home and wrote up a proposal to send to the publisher and I properly "ADHD'd it". I missed out loads of information because I just **had** to get it done and submitted as soon as I could.

Because I am so impulsive, I am also incredibly impatient. I hate waiting for anything! I am usually quite a passive person, but I hate waiting in queues, and being stuck behind a slow driver turns me into a road rage-filled bitch! To get to the point, which I know you will appreciate, when you have ADHD, waiting is, on occasion, torture.

> "My lack of patience has seen me leave many shop queues as I refuse to wait. I have put off contacting my GP as I can't bear phoning to try to get an appointment, so will go without."

LESLEY

> "Once, when I was at university, I was sitting in the stair well, waiting to use the communal phone (it was the '90s, pre-mobile phones). I had been waiting for nearly an hour, and I was beyond bored and fidgety. I happened to be sitting next to a fire alarm, the type with a 'Break glass for emergency' cover and a small hammer attached with a chain. It had grabbed my attention and I thought, 'I wonder how hard you have to actually hit the glass for it to break?' I'm sure you can imagine what happened next... The answer is 'surprisingly hard', but I was persistent and succeeded in getting the whole building evacuated, much to my immediate terror."

RACHAEL

I think fast, talk fast, read fast, walk fast, drive too fast and act fast. This is not always a good thing.

In meetings, I get incredibly frustrated with people who are slow and methodical, or people who talk too much (which is a bit rich coming from me!). I won't say anything, but inside my head I am screaming, "**Just get to the effing point!!!!**" I regularly bemoan the fact that meetings could take half the time if people just said what needed to be said rather than faffing around with what I perceive to be unnecessary waffle and comments. This means that, for many of us, we can become easily frustrated with others and with ourselves.

IMPULSIVITY AND IMPATIENCE

"I often forget my brain works more quickly and makes links really efficiently, and I get frustrated people don't do things at my pace. This can lead to conflict which is hard. I find I often switch off from slow-paced conversations, either that or inside my head I'm shouting 'Speed up!' or 'Summarize!' or 'Get to the point!' Again, it's not great, depending on the person and situation."

CATHERINE

"Before my diagnosis, I'd already accepted I possessed zero patience and it was never going to change, but of course I had, at the same time, internalized it as simply another character flaw. After years of hating myself for an impossibly short fuse, I realized that it must be hardwired; I just didn't know why. What I did know is that I had tried everything in my power to contain it, to tame it, to intellectualize myself out of these explosive episodes, to no avail. My inability to contain my frustration in every area of life has plunged me headfirst into more hot water than I can recall. Picture a life filled with train wrecks and dumpster fires, oh, and for the record, I am fond of a burning bridge too!"

JODY

I hate long car journeys because I just want to get to the destination. I find the build-up to events hard because I just want them to happen, and I hate waiting for food in restaurants, for trains that are delayed or for people who are late. I feel myself getting really, really stressed, and sometimes I will cry because I find it so stressful.

My kitchen is full of partly used dieting aids and supplements, which I have bought impulsively because I am too impatient to diet and exercise and lose weight in a healthy way. (They don't work by the way, so save your money!)

> "I can only be patient for so long, then I get really impulsive. So I can decide I won't buy something, and be like that, but then my head thinks about it and thinks about it, and boom! In a moment's weakness, I buy it. Not great for the finances, not great in having to explain why there is another package arriving."

CATHERINE

I know in the past I have been too impulsive with trusting people. I have jumped too quickly into friendships and relationships and given too much of myself away. It is then incredibly hurtful and upsetting to find that people's intentions are not always as pure as mine, and I have been taken advantage of by people on numerous occasions.

IMPULSIVITY AND IMPATIENCE

In the past, I have got myself into financial trouble because I find it so hard to wait for things I want to buy, and I do not always read the small print on agreements.

Unfortunately, my impulsivity led to some rather dangerous and scary situations in my youth. (Impulsivity and people pleasing are **not** always a good combination!) Desperate to please others and too impulsive to think through the consequences, I would agree to things that were simply not safe, let alone sensible or even legal!

My husband often tells me to "just slow down", and although I know he is right, it is easier said than done. He also calls me "Arfur" because I start things, then get distracted or bored and move on to the next thing, so I leave "Arfur/half a" job done.

I am trying really hard to stop myself being so impulsive. Before I spend money on a purchase, I will try to ask myself if I really need it. I have even learned not to jump into friendships so quickly, and am learning to implement boundaries to protect myself. If I get stuck in traffic or a train is delayed, I try to tell myself it is out of my control, and regulate my anger with breathing exercises or distraction.

Although I admit that I have made many mistakes due to my ADHD, I now see this element of my neurotype as a strength. I love my super-fast brain, and understanding my ADHD has allowed me to curb my impulsivity. I see my brain as being like a wild horse (a bit like that racehorse that Miriam bought so impulsively), and it just took some work and compassion for me to tame it.

> "I think impatience is simply the frustration that occurs when we are prevented from acting on our natural instincts... It's like trying to hold back a wave – it's a futile endeavour. It's going to happen eventually, so everyone is better off if we just ride it out. The caveat is that you need to have that impulsivity underpinned by knowledge and a solid ability to assess risk. We spend so long teaching kids to inhibit their innate impulsivity that we never teach them to lean into it and simultaneously assess the risks."

IRIS

WHAT ELSE COULD HELP?

- ✓ When you feel impatient and stressed, try mindfulness, breathing or distraction techniques.
- ✓ Identify situations when you are likely to become stressed out by impatience, such as long meetings or journeys.
- ✓ Keeping your hands busy with fiddle toys or doodling may be helpful when you are feeling impatient and stressed.
- ✓ When you have an idea that you just **have** to do, write it down in a separate book or notepad.

IMPULSIVITY AND IMPATIENCE

Write down the pros and cons of your impulsive plan or idea.
- ✓ Then try to wait (I know this will be hard!); revisit it a couple of days later and see if it is still such a good idea.
- ✓ Discuss your impulsive ideas with a trusted friend or partner before you act on them.
- ✓ Be prepared for situations when you may have to wait by having things that will occupy your brain (e.g. audiobooks, games on your phone or puzzle books).
- ✓ If you are finding it hard to concentrate or focus in long meetings, explain beforehand that you will need regular movement breaks.
- ✓ Plan ahead for long journeys with playlists and audiobooks, and take regular breaks.
- ✓ Remind yourself that there is a reason that you are prone to impulsiveness. Mentally telling yourself to stop, slow down, "it's just my wonky thalamus here", may help you think before you act.
- ✓ Similarly, your need for a dopamine hit could be redirected to something safer and less expensive if you are an impulsive spender (there is lots more information on this in Chapter Ten).
- ✓ If possible, avoid the environments or situations that trigger your impulsive behaviour.
- ✓ Recognize that you may be more impulsive when you are bored or under the influence of alcohol.
- ✓ Don't beat yourself up when you act impulsively with less than positive effects. Clock it down to experience and try to remind yourself of this the next time you feel like you have to do something **right now**!!!

Chapter Nine

Special Interests, Obsessions and Random Collections

It is pretty well understood that people who are autistic develop very strong and intense special interests, sometimes referred to as obsessions (which I don't like, as I think that sounds pretty negative) or hyperfixations. But it is not just autistic individuals who have special interests. As an ADHDer, I also have special interests and can get pretty obsessed with things, people, places, events, etc.

Spending time on our special interests is incredibly dopamine-fuelling. It can also be expensive as our special interests can be rather short-lived, but we don't usually lose interest until we have purchased all the kit or things we need to become an expert in our new-found hobby!

I can spend hours on my special interests, and sometimes they can become all-consuming. Some of my special interests include:

- The Titanic
- 9/11 and other terrorist attacks
- Serial killers
- Tudor history
- Conspiracy theories
- Doll's houses and miniatures.

When I am watching TV, I may become fascinated by an actor, and then spend hours researching them and watching everything they have ever been in.

I can lose myself for hours and hours reading, researching

online and going down lots of rabbit holes; this is where my "time blindness" really kicks in and I can lose hours mindlessly scrolling on the internet!

As women with ADHD, our interests can remain intense and last, or they may be intense but fleeting, because we lose the dopamine hit and get bored easily.

> "I do tend to cycle through some more short-lived fixations alongside deeper interests, and that can be anything from learning to play the ukelele to finding out about quantum physics! I used to hate the way I cycled through things and got bored before I'd learned something in any depth. Now I love the rabbit holes my brain takes me down, and I just go with it!"
>
> AMY

I think that obsessions have been most difficult when they are about people I know or have met. It is not that I have developed a romantic or sexual attraction to them; I just become really fascinated with them and want to learn as much as I can about them. I can imagine it could appear a bit "stalkerish" if the person found out I was so interested in them!! Interests in people seem quite common for us ADHD folk.

> "I found that I tended towards infatuation with people, especially during my younger years. It became a bit of a hyperfocus and I would put a lot of effort into getting the attention of the person that I was interested in."
>
> SARAH B

As I mentioned in Chapter Five, individuals with ADHD are highly monotropic, and our ability to hyperfocus and research can really come into its own when we are able to focus on our special interests.

When I get obsessed with things, people or events, there is nothing I like more than having someone I can share this with.

A couple of years ago, my husband and I accidentally discovered the beautiful town of Ludlow in Shropshire. I have always had a real fascination with old buildings and houses (particularly Tudor and Elizabethan), so I was extremely happy to find myself in the town with one of the highest number of listed building in the UK. (Yes, I researched it after we left!)

At first, my husband was a bit embarrassed as I kept stopping to take photos in the middle of the busy streets, but after a while, he started to point out some buildings for me to photograph, and showed an interest in reading the blue plaques to see how old they were, who had lived there, etc.

As soon as Steve did this, I felt an immediate rush of happiness that he was sharing my interest, and I instantly felt we were more connected. It was like a double dose of dopamine, and also really validating that my special interest was being shared and respected.

Luckily, another special interest of mine is neurodiversity, so I am very fortunate to have found myself in a career that is completely based on this. Most of my friends who are neurodivergent have found themselves working in an area that is somehow linked to their special interests. I simply cannot imagine doing a job that was outside of this, and as I said in Chapter Five, I think for an ADHDer, it just would not be conducive to a happy career.

> "For me, my special interests or fixations are psychology and (conveniently) all things neurodivergent! This has been fantastic for me as I made a career out of it by becoming a counsellor and then later specializing in neurodivergence. I never tire of the subject and I love finding out what makes people tick, so it's been the perfect vehicle for me to find my passion!"

AMY

Another reason special interests are so important to me is that they are a way that I can stop myself from becoming bored. Being bored is something I simply cannot tolerate. (I can't even tolerate standing still to brush my teeth!)

Some people look in their calendar and see gaps and time off and think how fortunate they are to have a break. I see gaps in my calendar, and it makes me anxious. There are two reasons for this. First, as someone who is self-employed, I see empty diary space as time when I am not earning money; second, when I see a gap in my diary, I think to myself, "What the hell am I going to do with myself?!" I know I need quiet weekends at times, but I still have to do "something" with my time. It is so, so hard to switch off and do "nothing", and my brain simply won't allow me to do so.

When I am bored, that is when I am most at risk of seeking a dopamine hit and my impulse control goes out the window. It is when I am most likely to start internet shopping or rummaging around in the kitchen looking for snacks – anything to get that "hit" I need and relieve the unbearable feeling of boredom!

My special interests allow me to fill any downtime with activities that are enjoyable and stimulating without depleting too much of my energy.

Our special interests can be a great source of comfort, as our monotropic focus can block out and give us a break from the "noise" we experience as women with ADHD.

SPECIAL INTERESTS, OBSESSIONS AND RANDOM COLLECTIONS

> "I have had many fleeting special interests across my life – some lasted weeks, some lasted months. However, I have had one enduring special interest that has been with me my whole life – health/medicine. Anything medical brought me such comfort as a child. I watched medical documentaries, I read science encyclopaedias, I fantasized about needing medical procedures, I made crutches, I made 'plaster' and plastered my sister frequently. All my dolls were bandaged. I made up stories where people or I had minor injuries. It was pure escapism and comfort. I excelled at any health-related subject at school, and then studied nursing at university."
>
> **SARAH B**

Although special interests have numerous benefits to us neurodivergent women, they can have their disadvantages as well. Some of my special interests have been in my life for some time, while others have been transient, and expensive. My kitchen has an embarrassing number of gadgets that have been used once as a result of a fleeting interest in a particular cuisine or style of cooking. I have paid for and then not started professional courses, and have piles of books that I have ordered and then not read, or lost interest in halfway through.

I also find it really, really hard to throw things away, so when I actually finish a product, whether it's food or a beauty product, I get a feeling of satisfaction that I did not waste my money.

People with ADHD are more likely to become hoarders; this is linked to both our difficulties with both executive functioning and decision making.

> "I have periodic culls when I'm overwhelmed, where I throw out loads of things indiscriminately, and then periods of time where things don't get appropriately removed/let go of. I can't regulate and prioritize all the things that I see others doing, in keeping a tidy clutter-free and functioning home. So I'd say I'm in the middle, with the absolute capacity to become a hoarder."

LYNDSEY

> A 2021 study by Sharon Morein-Zamir et al., published in the *Journal of Psychiatric Research*, found that as many as one in five adults with ADHD exhibit clinically significant hoarding symptoms.

I have to force myself to throw things away, but when I do, I actually feel lighter. I enjoy taking unwanted things to my favourite charity shop, and I get a Gift Aid statement from one each year about much my donations have raised, which feels really good and gives me that dopamine hit I love.

> "Oh, my. Hoarding. I do have a tendency to hang on to things, usually for sentimental reasons, or because 'I might need this/use this/wear this someday'. As I have gotten older and started a family, I have learned to let go of a lot of material things from the past, but there are plenty of items that I still hang on to because I find that many random objects help me remember people, events, feelings, etc. Birthday and holiday cards are good examples – I can't seem to throw them away, and I usually feel awful when I do."
>
> STEPHANIE

I, too, seem to develop an emotional attachment to inanimate objects and tend to "humanize" my things. This is a phenomenon known as anthropomorphism. I felt guilty recently that I couldn't take all my summer dresses away on holiday with me, and made a mental promise that I would take the ones I left behind on my next holiday so they would not feel so left out. I feel guilty throwing things away for this reason, and also feel that I have wasted my money and not justified my spending if I don't keep things. This has resulted in me collecting a **huge** amount of "stuff" over the years, most of it shoved away in boxes or drawers, never to be seen again!

> "I find it hard to part with things as I seem to attach significance to everything. For example, I have birthday and Christmas cards going back over 25 years. I don't know what to do with them, but I can't throw them away, so they sit in a wardrobe waiting to be re-read one day, probably when I am putting off a task I don't want to do."

MIRIAM

If you follow any ADHD groups on social media, you have probably heard of "DOOM piles" or "DOOM boxes".

DOOM stands for "Don't Organize, Only Move", and is typical of how I "tidy" my house and organize my things. I simply can't get my head around organizing my stuff or throwing it away, so I just pile it up or shove it into drawers or cupboards. My house always looks pretty tidy until you open the cupboards and drawers!

I have started trying to block time to clear my rammed-full cupboards and drawers, and realize that half the stuff in there has hardly been used (if at all!). We recently (very impulsively) put our house on the market (for about six weeks), which motivated me to have a really good clear-out, and I actually felt as if a weight had been lifted when we recycled or threw away so much stuff.

My overspending has definitely decreased since I got my ADHD diagnosis, because I recognize so much better that

SPECIAL INTERESTS, OBSESSIONS AND RANDOM COLLECTIONS

I "want" things rather than "need" them. I can curb my spending and incessant need for "stuff"; I am still a work in progress in this regard, but I am getting there. I also seem to have a bit more money in my bank account, so I am trying to "hoard" my money instead of stuff I don't really need.

WHAT ELSE COULD HELP?

- ✓ Set yourself small goals when trying to de-clutter your home. Don't try to clear your house in one go; that goal is too big and you are unlikely to achieve it. Start by clearing one small drawer or cupboard at a time.
- ✓ A "body double" or trusted, non-judgemental friend can help you with de-cluttering and with some tough decisions about what you really need to keep.
- ✓ Selling unwanted things online or taking them to a charity shop will give you a little dopamine hit as you can make extra money or know you are giving to a good cause.
- ✓ If de-cluttering feels too overwhelming, there are professional de-cluttering services that can help you.
- ✓ Set a timer so you clear out a little at a time to avoid overwhelm.
- ✓ Try to put time aside regularly and make a plan for keeping your space tidy, clean and organized; so, for example, "I will clean my bathroom on a Saturday and

change my bed on a Sunday." This will create new habits that are, again, small and achievable.
- ✓ Create "micro habits". So, for example, every time you go upstairs, take one thing to put away, and every time you come downstairs, one thing to throw away.
- ✓ Explore new activities that don't involve buying or saving things but that still give you that dopamine hit/glimmers.

Useful links

Hoarding Disorders UK helps and supports people who are affected not only by hoarding and clutter but also chronic disorganization: https://hoardingdisordersuk.org

Hoarding Support provides information, support and advice for people who hoard and their loved ones: https://hoarding.support

HoardingUK is the only UK-wide charity dedicated to supporting people affected by hoarding behaviours: https://hoardinguk.org

Chapter Ten

Shopping (and Other Addictions)

For years, scientists have speculated that ADHD may be caused by a dopamine deficiency.

Dopamine is the neurotransmitter that works with our brain to give us feelings of pleasure and satisfaction. As ADHDers, we often go "dopamine hunting" because our brains don't produce enough, which can, at times, lead us down some rather destructive and expensive paths.

> "I develop obsessions and I get lost in them for ages. They come and go, they change and become forgotten. I've got various items around my home that relate to an obsession, where I've bought many items to go with it, and then become bored and moved on. Things like candle making, preserve making, balms and remedies, herbal teas, plant and vegetable growing, multiple books on various types of easy/quick cooking… It goes on, but you get my drift!"

LYNDSEY

I have used shopping as a way to get my dopamine hit for as long as I can remember, and I have always been a brilliant/terrible shopper. One of my friends once described me as "an advertiser's dream" because if I saw an advert for something I liked on TV or in a magazine, I would often then **have** to buy that product.

I saw an advert once for some purple loafers in a magazine and decided I absolutely **had** to have them. I managed to track a pair down to a shop in London and sent my poor mum (who worked in London at the time) across town in her lunch break to get them for me. They were absolutely beautiful, and I spent a lot of time admiring them, but I didn't really have the confidence or feet to carry them off, so I think I wore them twice, which resulted in a lot of guilt about the wasted money and my mum's wasted lunch break.

For so many of us with ADHD, shopping is a far too easy way to get that all-important dopamine hit we are craving.

> "Shopping gives me joy; it's the dopamine hit I need. I've bought brand-new cars without test-driving them or thinking about the financial impacts. It's currently January and I've got most of my Christmas shopping done; then I forget about what I've bought and stashed away, and then buy more Christmas presents. My son is four, and I get so carried away with online shopping and the dopamine hit that he's got clothes aged 9–10 in his wardrobe. My daughter has four winter coats; it's getting out of control."
>
> HAZEL-LEE

Before I went into teaching, I worked in sales and marketing, a job I despised. The only saving grace of this job was that the office was next to a huge Marks & Spencer. Every time I had a stressful, boring or difficult day, I would go out at lunchtime or when I had finished and buy something to make myself feel better. When my manager asked me what I did to help me manage my stress, I told her, "I buy myself new knickers!" She probably thought I was slightly mad or suffering from some sort of stress-related incontinence!

Since my ADHD diagnosis, I understand that my brain is looking for regular dopamine hits. I also now understand that my job in sales and marketing was not in any way linked to my passions and interests, which is so important to a person with ADHD. The reason I love my job so much now and work so hard is that I find it so interesting, and this is what keeps me focused and stimulated. Without this stimulation, I needed to get it elsewhere.

When my son was in surgery having a major operation, the nurses told me to "keep busy" and suggested I went to nearby Tooting and passed the time that way rather than sitting in the hospital watching the clock. I did not need asking twice and returned to the hospital laden down with Primark bags filled with goodies to cheer both Fin and me up. One of the nurses laughed when I returned to the hospital and said, "Wow – you have been busy!" as I created a Primark-themed home from home in our little corner of the ward.

Some people may think it odd that I went shopping while my son was in the operating theatre, but for a person with ADHD, we need to be busy and occupied mentally almost constantly, so my trip to the shops meant that I remained as calm and distracted as possible. Sitting and waiting is hard for anyone with ADHD at the best of times, and sitting and waiting in a hospital while your son undergoes neurosurgery would be almost impossible!

Like most people with ADHD, I get easily obsessed about things I think I need, and will spend hours hunting down things I have seen people wear on TV or in magazines. I also get obsessed with certain makes of clothes, which tends to run in themes, and my favourite pastime is charity shop shopping, where the bigger the bargain, the better. If I am bored, feeling down or stressed, or I don't have much to do at the weekend, my "go to" way to occupy my time has, in the past, been to hit the shops, often resulting in overspending and purchasing things I really don't need.

Tuning into your emotions and the link between these and your spending habits can be a really helpful way to curb your spending.

To illustrate the link between the way that my ADHD has shaped my spending and need for shopping, I will share with you "The tale of the missing black top" (which was the spark for this very book!). Not only does this tale highlight my propensity to impulse-buy, but it also shows the absolute lengths my ADHD takes me to when I really, really want something!

A little while ago, I went to spend the afternoon with my friend Eliza, AKA "Missing the Mark". After an afternoon of hard work, we decided to go into Brighton where we rewarded ourselves with a cocktail at The Ivy (we are classy ladies after all!).

One Porn Star Martini later, we left The Ivy and I immediately spotted a rather nice-looking boutique with the fatal word "SALE" plastered over the front window.

Not only was there a sale in this shop, but it was a **75% off sale**!!!!!!!!!!!!! (As I have already said, the bigger the saving, the bigger the dopamine hit!)

I tried on and bought a lovely jacket (that I definitely didn't need) and a very beautiful black silk camisole top to go with the other 50+ black tops that live in my wardrobe.

A few months after the purchase of these lovely items, I had a very important meeting in London. As always, I started to plan my outfit about five days in advance because my ADHD means it takes me that long to make a decision. "Oh," I thought, "I will wear that beautiful silk top I bought in Brighton."

I went to locate the top but couldn't find it, despite searching through my vast and rather messy wardrobe. Ah, I realized, it must be with the jacket I bought with it... It wasn't.

The following evening, I emptied my **entire** wardrobe looking for this top. This process took hours because I have so many clothes, and being ADHD means that there is not an awful lot of order to my wardrobe.

While looking for the top, I got distracted by items I had forgotten I had and started trying them on. I then accepted that I have **way** too many clothes, so I started an "eBay pile" and a "charity shop pile", which stayed in my room, and then the boot of my car, for months, as my ADHD meant I kept forgetting that they were there!

My ADHD also means that I don't sleep well at the best of times, and that night, after not being able to find my top, I hardly slept at all as my brain went into overdrive, frantically trying to remember when I had seen that top. It came to me in the middle of the night: "I must have taken it to Ludlow!" My husband and I had recently had a long weekend in Ludlow where I had taken about two weeks' worth of clothes and worn about a tenth of them.

The next day, I called the hotel and asked if they had a lost property department. I described the top, which was getting more beautiful and more expensive the more I thought about it. The young girl asked me to hold while she went off and looked for me. Ten minutes later, she came back on the phone. "Yes, we do have a ladies' black silk top!" she said. My heart leapt. "Is it a black silk shirt, size 16?" she asked, hopefully. My heart sank again. "No – that's not it," I sighed, and resumed my search in the bedroom, this time expanding the search into my husband's wardrobe, in case he had mistaken a black silk top for one of his t-shirts.

I then took every single jacket I owned from my wardrobe and looked under every single one, but still no top.

That night, I realized my life would not be the same if I didn't find this black silk camisole, but I was starting to lose hope. I needed to find...a replacement.

I spent the evening searching for "classic 100% silk vest top", but none of them were as beautiful as the one I had lost. Eventually, after looking at dozens of pale imitations, I settled on one and then spent some time looking for a discount voucher before finally hitting "Buy now".

Then I had a brain wave!!!!!! I went on to Google Maps and located The Ivy, Brighton, found the name of the street and Googled "ladies' clothes shops in Brighton".

I phoned the clothes shop as soon as I could in the morning, and explained my predicament. I needed the name of the top I had lost so that I could buy an exact replacement (even though I had just bought a pale imitation).

The lady I spoke to said that she was quite new, and that she thought it would be better for me to speak to a lady at their other branch, as she could probably help me.

I called the lady at the Hove branch, and she was lovely! Again, I explained my predicament and we had a really lovely chat for about 25 minutes about clothing we had loved and lost over the years. We both sat on the phone desperately trying to remember the brand name of my 100% silk vest top, which was getting more beautiful and more expensive by the day. "It's on the tip of my tongue," we both said several times to each other, while shouting random words (Seraphina!!) to each other, and then, "No, that's not it."

"Leave it with me," she said, "I will phone you back in a few hours, I just need to give my brain a break and it will come to me when I least expect it..."

About three hours later, my new friend called me back. "So, I tried really hard to remember but couldn't, so I eventually rang the store's buyer, and she said it must have been 'Kimono'." I was overcome with gratitude and promised to go and visit my new friend next time I was in the area. Then I got to work searching for "Kimono 100% silk vest top", but nothing resembled the top I had lost.

Eventually, I decided to give up. My obsession with finding the top started to fade and moved on to another obsession (buying a jersey halter-neck top like one I used to wear in the '90s for my holiday to Spain – I found one, by the way).

A few months later, it was my stepdaughter's baby shower. Outfit planned well in advance, I went to get my navy-blue ruched-sleeved jacket **and there was my top**!!!!!!!!!!!!!!!!!!!!!!!!!!!!!! I was overjoyed with happiness and immediately

SHOPPING (AND OTHER ADDICTIONS)

messaged all my friends who I had told about the missing top so they could stop worrying too.

I noticed that the name of top was Komodo, not Kimono, so that search had been futile, and it was not 100% silk (it's cupro).

I tried the top on. "Meh," my brain thought; it was not quite as spectacular as I remembered, but I was still very happy to be reunited with it.

A few days later, a very small, neat package was posted through my door; it was the "pale imitation", which I impressively decided I no longer needed (although I was tempted). The returns process was really complicated and required my husband to print out some forms and labels at work.

All in all, I reckon that the total hours spent trying to locate this top added up to about two days' work, which does then make my top very, very expensive!!

I can now recognize that buying stuff makes me feel better because I get that much-sought dopamine hit, but I also recognize that the "high" I get from shopping does not last very long, and usually leaves me with terrible buyer's remorse.

I can also now recognize that the "need" I have to buy things is largely driven by my ADHD brain and need for a dopamine hit. I can tell myself that this is what is driving my desire for things, rather than the thing itself, which has really helped me to curb my spending – **most** of the time.

As individuals with ADHD, waiting can be really, really hard. We need instant gratification and that dopamine hit **now**. But although it is hard, it can be really helpful to force yourself to **wait** (if you can!). If you still remember what it was you wanted to buy in a week's time, then ask yourself again if you really do need it. Or, if you are out shopping and see something you think you want, ask yourself if this really is something you cannot live without.

There have been times in my life when if you asked me what I have in my bank account to the nearest £500, I honestly could not tell you. I would live on my overdraft and was reckless with my student loan when I was at university (let's just say not much of it went on books!).

> Having ADHD makes you impulsive and impacts your executive functioning, so planning ahead and organization are also really hard. Research funded by Monzo Bank and YouGov in 2022 found that people with ADHD are four times more likely to impulse-buy than those without ADHD. If we see something we want, we go for it immediately because we don't think about the sensible option of saving our money for future and more important bills and events.

"I have also realized recently how insidious online shopping is for someone like me; it latches firmly on to the part of my brain that fixates, and once my head is infiltrated, the 'must have' mindset finds it hard to relinquish control, locked into the doom scroll. I lie to myself from the wings, 'This is just research, keep scrolling!' I stop only when I am completely drained or I have given in to the purchase in spite of myself; it's the powerless nature of the pursuit that demoralizes so much. The more I learn about ADHD, the more I can spot the dangerous patterns of behaviour; I call it the 'slide'. So I am beginning to better identify the descent, and that gives me more opportunity to step back from those self-destructive choices and simply take a moment."

JODY

As I have got older, and particularly since being diagnosed and understanding my ADHD, I have developed a new obsession that is far more positive, and that is saving money. I actually get my dopamine hit from **not** buying something, or putting it back and walking away. When I am shopping online, I can get to the basket, then talk myself out of spending and click out of a website, and that feels really good!

I also like to set myself a challenge of not buying any clothes for a period of time, and when I have completed the challenge, this gives me a little hit that I need. This may not work for everyone with ADHD, but it has really worked for me for short periods.

I think if I had known I had ADHD when I was younger, this would have really helped me with my shopping addiction and overspending. Understanding my brain has not only helped me understand myself and feel better about myself, but has also saved me a lot of money too!!

I now understand that, like many people with ADHD, I have a **very** addictive personality. Some of the triggers for addiction include financial and relationship stress and boredom, which are common for those of us with ADHD.

> "I have had some unhealthy obsessions. I have always experienced some degree of disordered eating; this ties in with a sometimes-unhealthy relationship with exercise. I have to closely watch how much time I spend doing things because I can move into addictions and obsession quite quickly. For instance, games such as Wordle or Candy Crush can steal a huge amount of my time, energy and focus. Usually, I am all or nothing. I will play games until I realize how hard it is for me to do other things, so then I quit altogether. There is not often a middle ground."

SARAH B

SHOPPING (AND OTHER ADDICTIONS)

Common addictions for ADHD also include eating, alcohol, exercise, drugs and sex.

During my raving days, I developed a reputation for being "the last woman standing" and required "assistance" to be able to do this, mainly in the form of "speed"/amphetamines. I don't believe that I was addicted to drugs, but I was addicted to staying up for as long as possible.

After every rave or night out, there was always some sort of after-party, and I was always up for it. I think I was using raving as a form of escape, and admitting defeat and going home to my bed meant I was having to go back to reality, but this did start to lead me down a very slippery slope.

> I count myself lucky that although I have flirted with all of the above, my obsessions and addictions have not led me down far more destructive paths, but for some people with ADHD, this has not been the case. In March 2022, Peter Jaksa wrote an article in *ADDitude Magazine* that stated, "The lifetime occurrence of substance use problems among adults in the general population is approximately 25 percent. They may be addicted to alcohol, recreational drugs, or prescription medications. In comparison, 50 percent of adults with ADHD have a history of dealing with substance use at some point in their lives."

> Sadly, but not surprisingly, children with ADHD are more likely to start experimenting with alcohol than their neurotypical peers. A study by Barkley et al. in 2002, which followed children diagnosed with ADHD and a control group of children for eight years, found that at a mean age of 14.9 years, 40% of the ADHD children had tried alcohol compared to 22% of their neurotypical peers.

When we factor in the number of undiagnosed children, you can see that there is a potential ticking timebomb of addiction and substance misuse in later life. This is just one of the reasons why earlier diagnosis and understanding of neurodiversity is essential. I am not saying that knowing you have ADHD would prevent your addictions – addiction is far more complex than that – but knowing that your brain is seeking a dopamine hit could help you seek it out in less harmful ways.

As I have mentioned in other chapters, social situations can be really hard for people with ADHD. We may appear confident and can be great fun to be around at a party, but our RSD and imposter syndrome can mean that we mask in social situations, or, as I used to do, use alcohol to boost our confidence and get us over the threshold of social events. This can set up a cycle of "needing" alcohol to be able to socialize, lulling us into the belief that we can only do it with the crutch of alcohol there to support us.

"I have had an unhealthy relationship with alcohol for my whole adult life. From my mid-teenage years onwards, I have used alcohol as an attempt to 'fit in', to help my crippling social anxiety and communication difficulties and to self-medicate. In more recent years, as a parent of a child with complex additional needs, I drank to 'reward' and numb myself after difficult days, but every day was difficult, and I was habitually drinking every night."

RACHAEL

"The biggest thing I've learned over the last few years about myself and ADHD is definitely my use of alcohol, enjoying the feeling of 'not being me', and it being a coping mechanism in high-anxiety situations. If I enjoy something, I need it all the time. Impulsive buying different flavours of alcohol when I see it, and then because it's in the house I will drink it. I truly understand how years of being undiagnosed ADHD and not knowing about it has led to self-medication with alcohol in general as a way to cope with life."

MADDIE

> An article by Stephanie Watson, published by WebMD in 2022, stated that "ADHD is five to 10 times more common among adult alcoholics than it is in people without the condition. Among adults being treated for alcohol and substance abuse, the rate of ADHD is about 25%."

Since I have had my ADHD diagnosis and understand my brain so much better, I have stopped putting myself in situations where I need alcohol to feel comfortable. I have learned to say "no thank you" if I don't feel completely comfortable entering a social environment where I know the temptation to drink will be too much. I now have a "rule" that I don't drink on weekdays, and when I do drink, I try to do it more moderately. It doesn't always work, but I feel that I can control the drinking now more than it controls me.

I also have a much better understanding of the fact that a lot of the things I think I "need" I really don't – I just "want" them, and the dopamine fix they give me is just that, and it doesn't last. Understanding ourselves, our ADHD and our need for a dopamine fix can be incredibly helpful in maintaining healthier relationships with the things we are sometimes drawn to that can have negative impacts on our mental health and our physical health, and our wallets.

"Last year, I came across a particular approach for how to regain control over alcohol (rather than allowing it to control you). I began learning about the science behind alcohol and how clever marketing and social conditioning had had me hooked. I came to understand that alcohol was actually adding to my difficulties, not helping them. And once I realized how much I was 'being controlled' by the alcohol industry and social norms, I wanted to reject it all. I stopped drinking nine months ago, and, with the exception of a glass on a special occasion, I intend to stay this way."

RACHAEL

"The more I learn about ADHD, the more I can spot the dangerous patterns of behaviour; I call it the 'slide'. So I am beginning to better identify the descent, and that gives me more opportunity to step back from those self-destructive choices and simply take a moment. It's not a fool proof system – God knows this fool trips up time and time again, but never a truer word spoken than knowledge is power."

JODY

WHAT ELSE COULD HELP?

- ✓ Recognize your triggers (e.g. boredom, sadness, anxiety) and tune into these before you make impulsive decisions. Try to find other ways to manage these emotions. It can also be helpful to find patterns behind the behaviour. What causes you to spend, drink, eat, etc.?
- ✓ Avoid environments such as the shops, pub, etc. when you are experiencing the emotions that can lead to you engaging in dopamine-seeking and addictive behaviours, and try to find something else to do that gives you the relief and the dopamine hit you need.
- ✓ Distract yourself with something else; it could be a walk, exercise, phoning a friend, listening to music, etc. Recognize your need for a dopamine hit. Tell yourself that this is what your brain is needing, not the purchase, drink or food itself.
- ✓ Ask yourself if your purchase, food, drink or behaviour is a "need" or a "want". Can you actually justify the need? For example, are you replacing something you have lost, broken or actually require? Stop and think! Ask yourself why you are about to reach into your wallet or engage in the potentially harmful behaviour.
- ✓ When you go shopping or out for dinner or drinks, set yourself a realistic budget. Take cash out with you and leave your credit cards at home. Say "no" to store cards and credit cards! They are absolutely lethal and make overspending far, far too easy.

SHOPPING (AND OTHER ADDICTIONS)

- ✓ Banking apps and spending trackers can also help us visualize how much we are spending on things – often we don't realize how much we are spending on the "little things" as it is just so easy to tap a card or phone against a machine.
- ✓ Fill shopping baskets online or start wish lists – it's like window shopping online and can still be a little hit of excitement. Set yourself a challenge of not buying anything you don't need for a certain period of time, and then reward yourself with something (not too expensive, though! Like a meal out with a friend or a trip to the cinema). Tell someone about your challenge – so you are more likely to stick to it!
- ✓ Operate a one in, one out system. If you buy something, tell yourself that you have to take a similar item to a charity shop. If clothing is your shopping kryptonite, clear out your wardrobe regularly. I have items I have forgotten I own and have bought items of clothing only to realize I already own something almost identical!
- ✓ Don't set yourself unrealistic goals. For example, instead of saying, "I am not drinking at all for six months", say to yourself "I am going to only drink at weekends" or "I am going to stick to three drinks when I go out". You are more likely to stick to this rather than think, "Sod it, I may as well not even try!"
- ✓ Sometimes the triggers of your addictions may be linked environments, and this includes the people in it, so it may be that you have avoid these. You could

- suggest to a friend who may trigger your drinking that you meet in the day for a coffee instead of in the evening for drinks.
- ✓ If you feel like your addictions are controlling you rather than the other way round, it may be time to seek help. Start with one person you know well and trust; this could be a partner, friend or GP. The first step is usually the hardest to take, but it is also the most important one.
- ✓ A neuro-affirming therapist or counsellor may be able to help you with your addictive behaviours and unpick the underlying reasons and triggers.
- ✓ Find support with those who get it. This could be with close friends, online or in-person support groups.
- ✓ Lastly, don't beat yourself up if you slip up. Try to find that trigger of why you engaged in addictive behaviours, and tune into this the next time you are tempted.

Useful links

Addiction

AA (Alcoholics Anonymous), where alcoholics help each other: www.alcoholics-anonymous.org.uk

Help for Addiction ensures you receive the right support, whether you are dealing with addiction yourself or a friend, family member or loved one has an addiction: www.help4addiction.co.uk

Mind also has useful information on addiction: www.mind.org.uk

UK Rehab has information on many types of addiction, including shopping: www.uk-rehab.com

Debt

Citizens Advice: www.citizensadvice.org.uk

StepChange provides the UK's most comprehensive debt advice service: www.stepchange.org

Chapter Eleven

Dropping the Disorder and Reframing My ADHD

ADVENTUROUS

Determined

HARDWORKING

DEDICATED

Hopefully, if you are reading this, you have made it through the rest of the book (or maybe you just skipped to this last chapter, which I am prone to do).

However, you made it here, and I hope you now have a

better understanding of ADHD, and, more importantly, a better understanding of yourself.

I hope that some of the anecdotes from me and the other women who contributed to this book have made you feel less alone.

I hope you have had lots of "lightbulb" moments, and can now understand how your ADHD has an impact on you and your life.

I hope you feel validated, and feel that you are good enough as your true authentic self.

Most importantly, I hope you now realize that you are not disordered and not deficient in any way. You just have a brain that sometimes works too fast and tricks you into believing things about yourself that are not true.

If someone offered me a cure for ADHD, I would honestly tell them where to go (very politely, of course, because I still have those people-pleasing tendencies!).

Of course, my ADHD has sometimes made life trickier, but my ADHD is also responsible for some of the best decisions I have made, and gives me the energy and passion I have to make me successful too. After all, ADHD gave me the drive I needed to write this book.

Without doubt, the best thing I ever did was get my diagnosis and validate what I have always known.

Understanding my brain has made my life easier to navigate.

I can advocate for myself, and I value myself and my feelings far more.

I can recognize when my brain is needing a dopamine hit, and try to curb the behaviours that result from that.

I can tell when my brain is tricking me into thinking negatively about myself.

I can create boundaries when needed, and keep myself safe.

If I could go back in time, equipped with what I know about myself now, and do some things differently, I would.

If I could write my younger self a letter, this is what it would say:

> Dear Laura,
>
> I know that at times you think that you are not quite good enough. You often feel like you don't really fit in, that you are clumsy, forgetful, disorganized and a bit weird. You worry a lot about doing things that other people seem to be able to do effortlessly.

You feel that you are annoying at times, and that people don't really like you. You worry that you let people down, and that your best is not quite good enough.

You don't think you are cool, or pretty, or clever, and at times you are overwhelmed by self-consciousness and self-doubt.

You have been told you are "oversensitive" and so you spend a lot of time holding in your tears and true feelings.

You don't always like the way people treat you, and the way that you let them.

You worry that you find it hard to stick at things, and that you will never really find your true role in life.

You don't always know who the "real" Laura is or how you should just "be".

I want to tell you that when you are older, you will find the "real" Laura and you will really, really like what you find.

You will have a successful career, doing something you love.

You will have a happy marriage, with someone who loves you for your true authentic self.

You will be the most amazing mum to the most amazing young men.

DROPPING THE DISORDER AND REFRAMING MY ADHD

You will have a fantastic group of friends who love and accept you for being the "real you".

You will find out that you are ADHD. It will change your life, and you will understand that you are not:

- Clumsy
- Stupid
- Forgetful
- Annoying
- Disorganized
- Oversensitive
- Lazy
- And generally, a bit of a walking disaster.

Instead, you will understand that you are:
- Adventurous
- Determined
- Hardworking
- Dedicated.

Finally, and although you will still have your challenges, you will understand that you are more than good enough as you are.

Love,

Your future self xx

HARDWORKING

"I'd tell myself that there are major reasons as to why I have forever felt 'different', and most importantly, that these differences are not because I am 'broken'. They are because I am wired differently. This is something to celebrate...but I am still working on this. Surround yourself with like-minded people, join the groups and read positive material. Keep trying to fit things into your busy life that make you, you! Without them, you feel like an imposter trying to be grey in a very colourful world! Try to connect with your neurodiversity rather than turn your back on it. It is only through self-acceptance that we can be authentically ourselves... like I say, though, I am working on it!"

BETHANY

DEDICATED

"As hard as it is and as cheesy as it is, if you're a masker like I am, unleash the mask and be the fun, caring, extremely humorous person that you are, and don't question yourself while being this way. You'll eventually find your tribe. It is extremely important to have people that 'get you'! It's only now at 43 that I'm starting to realize this fact, and say it quite a bit to my eldest daughter about 'finding your tribe'.

KATE

Determined

"Look into it – seek out information about how ADHD presents in women, especially from ADHD women and parents with lived experience, and if you feel it resonates with your own experience, then speak to your GP about a referral. Don't be gaslit by other people in your life or medical professionals – you know yourself better than anyone else. And be kind to yourself, show yourself compassion – this is hard, really hard sometimes, and you're doing the best you can. It sounds cliché, but it's so true."

COURTNEY

HARDWORKING

"I am not diagnosed, but I know at least one if not both my boys have ADHD. I have realized it may apply to me. It makes sense of much of my life. If I had known, I feel it would have helped me to prepare myself for the difficulties I faced. It would have allowed me to be kind to myself on those days where I struggled instead of feeling like I'm failing at being a good mum and partner, and not understanding why I couldn't do simple tasks. I could have just allowed myself to go easy and break things down."

SARAH M

Determined

"I've thought hard about how I used to see myself, but it's blurry as I think I was in a fog of RSD overdrive fuelled by 'gaslighty' drivel and onion layers of trauma. Now my vision and my internal dialogue is clear. I hold my head up and walk with pride that I get so much shit done! My anxiety drives me, my hyperfocus pumps my veins. My intuition keeps those 'gaslighty' delights outside of my dance space. I laugh at my meandering articulation and own it with honour. Take me or leave me, your choice. Others' judgement is no longer any of my business."

MICHELE

DEDICATED

"Be kind to yourself and accept help from others if it's available. No one person has to do it all and be it all."

KELLY

Determined

"You aren't alone, and you are doing the best you can. Just because you have intrusive thoughts doesn't mean you want to act on them or that they are how you really feel. If you really were a bad parent, you wouldn't care about this in the first place. DOOM boxes are your friend, and placing things with other things to help you remember can really help. Put things you know you struggle to remember with things you have to use on a daily basis; for example, I place my vitamins next to my deodorant. If you are struggling mentally, talk to someone – there is no shame in asking for help and having talking therapy. If you become overstimulated by noise from the children, then invest in some noise-cancelling earbuds/headphones; this was a game-changer for me. As long as you are in the same room as them to watch them, then this is a great tool I find really useful. Also with fidget toys, I found it difficult to know which ones worked for me. A lot of them frustrated me and made me cross until I explored a wider range and found I liked fidget spinners and a snake puzzle. So definitely explore various ones to see if they help. Fidget jewellery is great for when in public too."

LAUREN

ADVENTUROUS

"My own lack of patience for 'normal' life took me to the last frontier, living in a bush cabin, running sled dogs and hanging out with crazy Alaskans. I learned what it feels like to be in the presence of a landscape older than the human mind can comprehend, and it is painfully, immediately obvious that you are inconsequential to its existence, and it feels good to be made small by such things. This and this alone quieted my mind for the first time ever. In this vast wilderness, I was also patient, resilient and determined. If I made a mistake, it was simply a teacher; it was not a reason to get angry, because impulsivity in this part of the world can kill, and you feel that jeopardy more keenly than any rising frustration. In a place where the 'normal' rules of society didn't exist, where wits and will were required, my hunter-gatherer brain excelled, and despite being decades away from diagnosis, this profound experience of kinship with people and place gave birth to a sense of belonging I'd never felt before. This new feeling was a foundation of peace, like a chink of light in the darkness, a notion that I was finally worth something. I realize now, post diagnosis and armed with so much more understanding than before, that in some weird paradox my impulsive adventures became my own salvation, the beginnings of what we might call 'self-acceptance'; would I ever have found that in a suburban nine-to-five existence, who can say?"

JODY

Determined

"Now I am increasingly finding my neurodiverse tribe of friends and work colleagues (and have many existing friends who are neurodiverse – either diagnosed or undiagnosed but researching themselves), I feel as if I can be myself far more. I am naturally quite quiet and, dare I say, 'boring', but I am happy with this aspect of myself, and if others don't like it, then that's their problem! With my neurodiverse friends, I also feel safe to be my slightly wackier, fun-loving self, too. It's a win-win!"

KATIE

HARDWORKING

"Finding other ADHD folks who had very similar struggles and stories to my own – it was a revelation. I wasn't broken beyond repair, I wasn't this terrible, cursed person. I wasn't all of the negativity that I had taken into myself over 30 years. I was ADHD. I had spent so long beating myself up for being unable to meet a neuronormative standard that I would never be able to attain – for living without the appropriate support and medication I needed. I started to be kinder to myself. That when I could accept it, it was okay to ask for help rather than struggle – that didn't make me any lesser."

KYRA

I hope you now realize that you are not broken, weird, deficient, lazy or any other of the words that you may have used to describe yourself, and I have I left a space now in this book for you to write your younger self a letter too.

References

ADHD UK (2023) "ADHD incidence." https://adhduk.co.uk/adhd-incidence

ADHD UK (2024) "ADHD UK - Percentage diagnosed vs undiagnosed." https://adhduk.co.uk/adhd-diagnosis-rate-uk

Andersson, A., Garcia-Argibay, M., Viktorin, A., Ghirardi, L. et al. (2023) "Depression and anxiety disorders during the postpartum period in women diagnosed with attention deficit hyperactivity disorder." *Journal of Affective Disorders* 325, 817–823. https://doi.org/10.1016/j.jad.2023.01.069

Barkley, R.A., Fischer, M., Smallish, L. and Fletcher, K. (2002) "The persistence of attention deficit hyperactivity disorder into young adulthood as a function of reporting source and definition of the disorder." *Journal of Abnormal Psychology* 111, 2, 279–289.

Clance, P.R. and Imes, S. (1978) "The impostor phenomenon in high achieving women: Dynamics and therapeutic intervention." *Psychotherapy Theory, Research and Practice* 15, 3. www.paulineroseclance.com/pdf/ip_high_achieving_women.pdf

REFERENCES

Constance, L. (2021) "Study: Children with ADHD more likely to bully – and to be bullied." *ADDitude*, 3 January. www.additudemag.com/bullying-and-adhd-research

D'Arrigo, T. (2020) "Endometriosis, psychiatric disorders may raise the risk of one another." *Psychiatric News* 55, 9. https://doi.org/10.1176/appi.pn.2020.4b10

Dana, D. (2018) *Polyvagal Theory in Therapy: Engaging the Rhythm of Regulation*. W. W. Norton & Company.

Dodson, W.W. (2016) "Emotional regulation and rejection sensitivity." https://chadd.org/wp-content/uploads/2016/10/ATTN_10_16_EmotionalRegulation.pdf

Dorani, F., Bijlenga, D., Beekman, A.T., van Someren, E.J. and Kooij, J.S. (2021) "Prevalence of hormone-related mood disorder symptoms in women with ADHD." *Journal of Psychiatric Research* 133, 10–15. https://doi.org/10.1016/j.jpsychires.2020.12.005

Hergüner, S., Harmancı, H. and Toy, H. (2015) "Attention deficit-hyperactivity disorder symptoms in women with polycystic ovary syndrome." *The International Journal of Psychiatry in Medicine* 50, 3, 317–325. doi: 10.1177/0091217415610311.

Jaksa, P. (2022) "The ADHD & addiction link: Addictive behaviors in adults explained." *ADDitude*, 31 March. www.additudemag.com/addictive-behaviors-adhd

Klefsjö, U., Kantzer, A.K., Gillberg, C. and Billstedt, E. (2021) "The road to diagnosis and treatment in girls and boys with ADHD – gender differences in the diagnostic process." *Nordic Journal of Psychiatry* 75, 4, 301–305. doi: 10.1080/08039488.2020.1850859.

Kooij, J.J.S. (2019) "Is ADHD a circadian rhythm sleep disorder? & relationship with health." ADANA, Barcelona, 10 May.

https://adanajornadas.org/pdf/2019/TDAH%20y%20edad%20adulta%20Sandra%20Kooij.pdf

Malapani, C. and Fairhurst, S. (2002) "Scalar timing in animals and humans." *Learning and Motivation* 33, 1, 156–176. https://doi.org/10.1006/lmot.2001.1105

Morein-Zamir, S., Kasese, M., Chamberlain, S.R. and Trachtenberg, E. (2021) "Elevated levels of hoarding in ADHD: A special link with inattention." *Journal of Psychiatric Research* 145, 167–174. doi: 10.1016/j.jpsychires.2021.12.024.

Murray, D., Lesser, M. and Lawson, W. (2005) "Attention, monotropism and the diagnostic criteria for autism." *Autism* 9, 2, 139–156. doi: 10.1177/1362361305051398. https://monotropism.org/murray-lesser-lawson

NICE (National Institute for Health and Care Excellence) (2024) "Attention deficit hyperactivity disorder: How common is it?" Clinical Knowledge Summaries. https://cks.nice.org.uk/topics/attention-deficit-hyperactivity-disorder/background-information/prevalence

Porges, S.W. (1995) "Polyvagal Theory." www.stephenporges.com

Prasad, D., Wollenhaupt-Aguiar, B., Kidd, K.N., de Azevedo Cardoso, T. and Frey, B.N. (2021) "Suicidal risk in women with premenstrual syndrome and premenstrual dysphoric disorder: A systematic review and meta-analysis." *Journal of Women's Health* 30, 12. https://doi.org/10.1089/jwh.2021.0185

Sherman, C. (2019) "Is it ADHD, depression, or both?" *ADDitude*, 26 September. www.additudemag.com/adhd-and-depression-symptoms-treatment

Spencer, T., Biederman, J. and Wilens, T. (2004) "Nonstimulant treatment of adult attention-deficit/hyperactivity disorder."

REFERENCES

The Psychiatric Clinics of North America 27, 2, 373–383. doi: 10.1016/j.psc.2003.12.001.

Team Monzo (2022) "Living with ADHD can cost an extra £1,600 a year because of difficulties managing your money." Monzo, 27 June. www.monzo.com/blog/the-extra-costs-of-living-with-adhd

Watson, S. (2022) "ADHD and substance abuse." WebMD, 25 August. www.webmd.com/add-adhd/adhd-and-substance-abuse-is-there-a-link

Wikipedia contributors (2024) "Spoon theory." 26 September. https://en.wikipedia.org/wiki/Spoon_theory

Young, S., Adamo, N., Ásgeirsdóttir, B.B, Branney, P., et al. (2020) "Females with ADHD: An expert consensus statement taking a lifespan approach providing guidance for the identification and treatment of attention-deficit/hyperactivity disorder in girls and women." *BMC Psychiatry* 20, 404. https://doi.org/10.1186/s12888-020-02707-9